The Canal on the James
An Illustrated Guide to the James River and Kanawha Canal

T. Gibson Hobbs, Jr.

Compiled by Nancy Blackwell Marion

Edited by Mary Molyneux Abrams
and Thomas G. Ledford

BLACKWELL PRESS
LYNCHBURG, VIRGINIA

T. GIBSON HOBBS, JR. (1917–2005) was a native of Lynchburg, Virginia. He attended Lynchburg College and graduated with a degree in mechanical engineering from the University of Virginia. He served aboard the carrier U.S.S. *Enterprise* as an aircraft maintenance engineer during World War II and retired as a Lieutenant Commander, USNR. His civilian career was spent at Lynchburg Foundry Company and C.B. Fleet Pharmaceutical Company where he was vice president of manufacturing. A member of the American Canal Society and the Virginia Canals and Navigations Society, Gibson contributed many articles and commentaries about the James River and Kanawha Canal and its builders.

NANCY BLACKWELL MARION, owner of both The Design Group and Blackwell Press, is the publisher of *Lynch's Ferry* magazine. She has developed and maintains a virtual archive of Lynchburg—a database of photographs— for future generations to enjoy. Samples of her ongoing project can be seen at LynchburgHistory.com.

© 2009 by Blackwell Press

All rights reserved

Published 2009

All rights reserved. No part of this book may be reproduced in any form or by any electronic or mechanical means without permission in writing from Blackwell Press.

ISBN (soft cover): 0-9779523-3-9

Library of Congress Control Number: 2009924299

Printed in South Korea

Published by Blackwell Press, Lynchburg, Virginia

Contact Blackwell Press at:
311 Rivermont Avenue
Lynchburg, Virginia 24504
434-528-4665
Email: Sales@BlackwellPress.net
www.BlackwellPress.net

ON THE COVER:
Edward Beyer lithograph of the canal near Glasgow.
COURTESY TED TREVEY

View of the James River and Kanawha Canal in Richmond, Virginia
FROM A PHOTOGRAPH BY ANDERSON AND CO., RICHMOND

Contents

How it came to be	iv
Preface	v
Acknowledgments	vii
Engineering the Canal	1
Lynchburg and Its Canal Era	53
Canal Boats	71
Canaling on the Jeems and Kanawhy by Leighman Hawkins	89
Maps	97
Resources	162
Index	164

How it came to be

What I'm about to write can be taken as a tribute or as a cautionary tale. It is the story of how this book began.

It started with a simple inquiry. Nancy Blackwell Marion called T. Gibson Hobbs, Jr. to ask if he had any old photographs of Lynchburg: pictures from his boyhood, from his days at the foundry, or perhaps from his explorations on the James River.

Gibson said yes and invited Nancy to come take a look.

Nancy, the publisher of *Lynch's Ferry* magazine, is the owner of both The Design Group and the Blackwell Press. As a side project, she has developed and maintains a database of photographs and artifacts pertaining to the history of Central Virginia. A good part of this virtual archive can be accessed online at www.LynchburgHistory.com. Selected images also appear in Nancy's "Mystery Picture of the Week" column in Lynchburg's *The News & Advance*.

Gibson and Nancy first sat down together on a rainy Saturday afternoon, November 16, 2002. The meeting ended with the future author and future publisher frantically plucking slides out of the puddles in Gibson's driveway. One of several metal file boxes stuffed with a lifetime's worth of research had overturned on its way to the trunk of Nancy's car.

Nancy spent Saturday evening and Sunday morning carefully drying slides and putting them back in order according to Gibson's notes. Then, at 1:43 p.m. she began scanning images and typing in the corresponding text for each one. By the following Sunday, at 12:16 a.m., she had finished scanning, printing, and collating 400 of the 3000 slides in Gibson's collection.

When Gibson saw the result of Nancy's effort—an organized, indexed, full-color catalog of his work—he was thrilled and offered to pay Nancy to produce additional copies. Nancy said no. First of all, it was a volunteer project. Second, they weren't even close to being done.

Crafting a book is an off-putting task. Which is why Nancy never exactly proposed a book project per se. Hers was more of a "stone soup" approach. She would suggest, for example, that a catalog of pictures might be a lot tastier with more copy to support it. A chapter had the potential to be even more delicious with a corresponding series of maps to help illustrate it. A handful of portraits could use a pinch of captions, don't you think?

Before he knew it, Gibson was working on a book.

—Mary Molyneux Abrams

Preface

T. Gibson Hobbs, Jr. was our friend and a true friend of the James River and Kanawha Canal. He introduced most of us to the canal through his lectures and occasional articles, and many of us followed him out to the countryside to uncover and record the hidden relics of Virginia's greatest engineering adventure. It was his intention to write a book that would summarize more than three decades of research gleaned from libraries, archives, railway company files and the long abandoned locks and culverts along the right of way. When Gibson died in 2005, the book was largely done. We have merely pitched in to finish the job and make his great wealth of knowledge available to everyone as he intended.

A Lynchburg native, Gibson Hobbs grew up in Rivermont and explored the bluffs and banks along the James River with his neighborhood pals. He attended Lynchburg College and graduated with a degree in mechanical engineering from the University of Virginia. He served aboard the carrier U.S.S. *Enterprise* as an aircraft maintenance engineer during World War II and retired as a Lieutenant Commander, USNR.

After the war Gibson went to work for the Lynchburg Foundry Company, located on the banks of the James River. He moved over to the C.B. Fleet Pharmaceutical Company in 1961 and eventually became vice president of manufacturing. In Lynchburg he was an elder of First Christian Church and a trustee of Lynchburg College. As a member of the American Canal Society and the Virginia Canals and Navigations Society Gibson contributed many articles and commentaries about the James River and Kanawha Canal and its builders.

Gibson wrote the three sections of text included in this book at different times. Consequently, there were details that were inconsistent because he included new data as he found it. In general the book is derived from a series of lectures about the canal and the careers of its builders, which he presented to more than a hundred civic, professional and educational groups. The Lynchburg chapter of the American Society of Civil Engineers, the Lynchburg Historical Foundation, history classes at Central Virginia Community College, the Archeological Society of Virginia, the Lynchburg Exchange Club and the Kiwanis Club are just a few of the groups with whom he shared the story. The lectures span a period from the early 1970s through the late 1990s when his declining health made it difficult to get around. Each lecture benefited from Gibson's continuing research, and it has been our challenge to edit the book in a way that retained his style and emphasis but brought each section and caption up to the level of his latest research.

Gibson's goal was the preservation of every piece of evidence he could find that illuminated the history of the canal. He wanted this book to find its way into the hands of everyone who shared his interest and curiosity because he understood that public knowledge is the best way to save what is left.

—Thomas G. Ledford

T. Gibson Hobbs, Jr., Minnie Lee McGehee, and Dr. William Trout III at the 2003 Virginia Canals and Navigations Society meeting in Danville, VA..

Hundreds of friends helped Gibson clear trees and brush from the canal works. Without their efforts, this book would not exist. This photo was taken by John Taylor at locks 46 and 47.

Acknowledgments

Many people helped Gibson throughout the years and only he knew them all, but Theodore Haxall, Minnie Lee McGehee, and Dr. William Trout III stand out as colleagues and fellow contributors. Minnie Lee was an early editor and has been a persistent advocate for the book. In the six years that I have been working on it, she has gently prodded me toward a finished product. She read many proofs and contributed invaluable suggestions. Bill Trout helped tremendously with the technical aspects of the canal and contributed photos of the eastern end. Much of the information in the map section is derived from his famous river atlases. I could never have completed Gibson's work without the two of them.

Bringing this book to publication required the talent, goodwill, and advice of many people. I especially want to thank Darrell Laurant for smoothing out the syntax, Doug MacLeod for his knowledge of the James River, Emily Flint for annotating the maps, and Clifton Potter and Joyce Maddox who proofread. I have met many interesting people along the way and want to express my appreciation to Harry Gleason of the town of Buchanan, Chris Wiley of the Chesapeake & Ohio Historical Society, Mason Basten of the Virginia Canals and Navigations Society, and Robert K. Spencer, for the tour of Scottsville.

I owe a special debt of gratitude to Al Chambers. His breadth of knowledge is staggering, his editorial instinct is spot on, and his humor makes a grueling process bearable—even fun.

I waited several years for Tom Ledford to be able to check the facts on the ground in Lynchburg. If there is one person who knows the city's history, it is Tom, and I thank him for his guidance. It was worth the wait.

I wish to thank Mary Abrams for wrangling the text into manageable order. She has worked with me for years to make this the most complete and accurate record of the canal that we can create.

Finally, on behalf of everyone who cares about Gibson's legacy, I want to thank Peggy Hobbs for graciously supporting this effort. She never failed to open her home and welcome me inside, even though I often appeared on short notice and stayed too long.

Almost all of the illustrations in this book came from Gibson's slide collection and were used in conjunction with his lectures. Most were taken by him and then meticulously sorted and categorized. However, in some cases, he did not note the source. I have attempted to research and credit the photographer, artist, or owner of an image whenever possible. Many I believe are in the public domain, but I am sure there are still a few that I have neglected to properly credit. For that I apologize in advance, and hope that the benefit of getting the information into the hands of the public will outweigh unintended errors.

To all who helped, thank you.

—Nancy Blackwell Marion

Engineering The Canal

Construction of Orange & Alexandria Railroad bridge over the canal and river near Lynchburg. This sketch by Alfred Brown Peticolas shows the type of derricks used in erecting stonework of locks, dams, and culverts. These stone piers and abutments are still standing.
COURTESY VIRGINIA HISTORICAL SOCIETY

"Engineering the Canal" gathers all of Gibson Hobbs's research into a comprehensive narrative of the organization of the canal and profiles each of the major personalities involved in its construction and operation. It includes some of his earliest research, based on lectures he gave dating back to the 1970s, and benefits from his continuing work to uncover evidence as new materials became available during the last twenty years. This section is organized chronologically with sidebars and captions, emphasizing aspects that Gibson felt were significant. Revisions have been made for continuity.

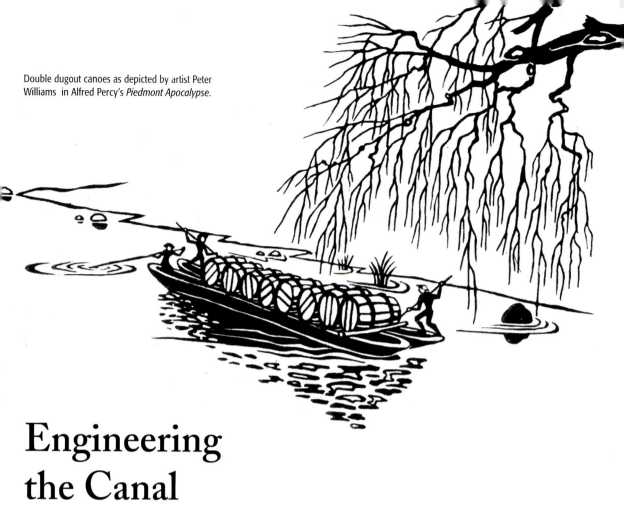

Double dugout canoes as depicted by artist Peter Williams in Alfred Percy's *Piedmont Apocalypse*.

Engineering the Canal

The Need to Reach the West

When George Washington made his sixth visit to what was then the American frontier in 1784, he returned even more excited about the prospects of the region.

In an October 10, 1784, letter to Governor Harrison of Virginia, Washington predicted that the area drained by the Ohio, James, and Kanawha rivers, particularly, would "be settled faster than anyone ever did, or any would imagine. . . . But smooth the road and make the way easy for them, and see what an influx of articles will be poured upon us; how amazingly our exports will be increased to them, and how amply we shall be compensated for any trouble and expense that we may encounter to effect it."

At that time, Virginia stretched from the Atlantic Ocean across the Alleghenies to the Ohio River. Coursing through the center of the state were the James and the Kanawha rivers, which Washington saw as potential highways uniting East with West.

Statue of George Washington, Rotunda, Virginia State Capitol
JEAN-ANTOINE HOUDON, 1785-1788

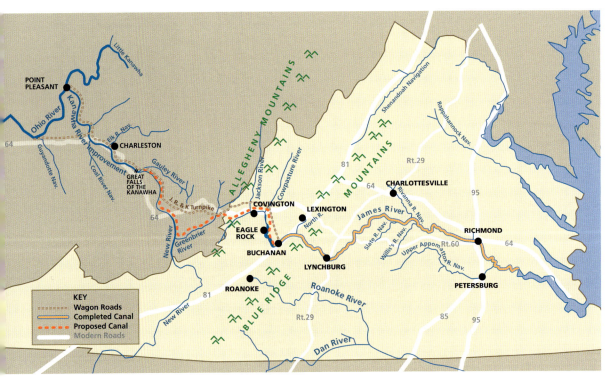

Map of canal route with the Kanawha Turnpike across the mountains to the Ohio River

The James, fed mainly by the Jackson and Cowpasture rivers, runs generally eastward through the Blue Ridge Mountains, then flows to the Chesapeake Bay. The Kanawha has more complex origins. At a spot southwest of present day Covington, the New River intersects with the Greenbrier River and continues its journey north from the North Carolina mountains. A little farther north, just above the great falls of the Kanawha, the Gauley River adds its volume to what then becomes the Kanawha. From the falls, the Kanawha continues on to join the Ohio at Point Pleasant, about 485 miles from Richmond. The Ohio flows into the Mississippi, which empties into the Gulf of Mexico.

As early as 1750 settlers had become established along the James above Richmond, all the way to the Blue Ridge Mountains. Others coming through the Shenandoah Valley from Pennsylvania were settling the upper reaches of the James. West of the Allegheny Mountains, there were only Indians, Indian traders, and explorers. Roads were poor or nonexistent in this back country, and small boats such as canoes and "double canoes" that plied the James River and its feeders offered the most practical means of moving goods to eastern markets and bringing in supplies.

After the 1760 defeat of the French, who had previously controlled the Ohio, more settlers began moving across the mountains into the Ohio River valley. In 1770 George Washington made his fifth journey to the Trans-Allegheny region, leaving Fort Pitt (now Pittsburgh) to boat down the Ohio and up the Kanawha on a mission of exploration. What he saw prompted his return fourteen years later, after the messy business of winning independence from Great Britain and forming a new government had been completed.

The Virginia General Assembly was impressed by Washington's letter to Harrison, and even more impressed by his personal visit to the nation's oldest state legislature in November of 1784. So on January 5, 1785, the Assembly chartered the James River Company to improve navigation on the James, with the ultimate aim of connecting its eastern commerce with that of the Ohio River. This was one of the earliest such efforts in the new America, and would later spawn state control of the James River Company and the 1835 formation of the James River and Kanawha Company.

The First James River Company

The 1785 charter for the first James River Company specified two tasks: to construct a canal for batteaux around the Falls of the James, through Richmond to Tidewater; and to improve the river for navigation as far west as practicable. It was agreed later that the upstream terminus of these improvements should be Crow's Ferry at the mouth of Looneys Creek, just above present-day Buchanan, about 200 miles above Richmond. These improvements would allow boats of one-foot draft to pass during the dry season, and tolls to be collected on all riverboat traffic.

The lure of profits from expected river commerce brought a ready sale of the stock, and the company was organized on August 20, 1785. A survey for the canal was made in 1786 by Eliot Lacy. In late 1789 the canal around the falls, although not complete, was open for business. It was in two parts, the Upper and Lower Canal, making it the first operating canal system with locks in the United States. George Washington took a batteau through it during his great tour of the South in 1791. The canal's terminus, the Great Basin in downtown Richmond, was opened in late 1800. Navigation improvements for batteaux were also made on the North River branch to Lexington and on the Rivanna

1785

George Washington took a batteau through the Lower Canal during his great tour of the South in 1791.
DETAIL OF A WATERCOLOR BY ART MARKEL
COURTESY BILL TROUT

In 1812, Chief Justice John Marshall headed a party of six to explore the route for the proposed canal over the Allegheny Mountains.

River branch to Charlottesville. A rough wagon road over the mountains also had been constructed.

River improvements consisted of cutting sluices through the rocky ledges of rapids and building wing dams to channel water into those sluices so boats could pass easily, even in the dry season. By 1808 river traffic had reached the point where the stockholders were realizing handsome dividends. Many and varied river craft, including flat-bottomed batteaux, were being poled up and down the James.

In his 1808 report to Congress on "Public Roads and Canals," Secretary of the Treasury Albert Gallatin said of the James River project: "The natural navigation of the river through that extent [from Richmond to Crow's Ferry] is considered better than that of any other Atlantic river above the falls."

Gallatin was concerned, however, that the Tidewater Connection in Richmond had not been completed, because it represented the least expensive way to get coal onto large vessels below the falls. Coal, he said, "is in no other part of the United States found in abundance in the vicinity of tide water."

The Secretary was referring to the mines then operating above Richmond. Little could he foresee that more than a century later tremendous rail traffic would haul coal along the James to Tidewater from the many mines farther west, in the mountains.

In a section of his report titled "Communications Between the Atlantic and Western Waters," Gallatin expressed dismay at the 3,000-foot height of the Allegheny Mountains. Since the highest canal in Europe then had a summit only 600 feet above sea level, he concluded that canal passage over the mountains was not possible. Again, he could not foresee the Erie Canal skirting the upper end of the Appalachian range, or the tunnels piercing through it. He felt the only answer was navigation as high as practicable on the eastern and western rivers, augmented by roads across the mountains.

In 1810 a contract was made with Ariel Cooley, a contractor from Springfield, Massachusetts, to build a series of thirteen wooden locks at Richmond to complete the connection to Tidewater, as required by the charter. These, however, were poorly constructed and soon deteriorated to such an extent that they were of little use. Meanwhile the James River Company was making exceptional profits but showed little interest in spending enough money to improve navigation further, or to improve the rough road over the mountains.

Largely because of the insistence of western interests, a commission of twenty-one members was appointed in 1812 to survey and report on improving the upper James and smoothing the connection across the mountains to the Kanawha River. Chief Justice John Marshall of Virginia headed a party of about six members who set off to explore the route. Leaving Lynchburg on September 2, they proceeded by boat up the James to Dunlaps Creek at Covington. Hauling the boat by wagon, they then followed the rough moun-

Batteaux had been used since 1771 to transport cargo from above Lynchburg to Richmond. River improvements consisted of cutting sluices through rocky ledges of the rapids, and in many cases wing dams were built to channel water into the sluices in the dry season. This drawing shows a batteau on the New River.
SCRIBNER'S MONTHLY, JANUARY 1873

tain road up the creek and over the mountains to strike the Greenbrier River just west of present-day White Sulphur Springs.

In spite of low water, they managed to reach the New River, negotiate its twenty-three-foot falls, and float down the river to the Kanawha Falls. The surveyor, Andrew Alexander, recorded distances, elevations, and obstructions for each part of the route. Abandoning the batteau at Kanawha Falls, the party returned by land to Lynchburg arriving about November 1.

Because of the intervention of the War of 1812, the report of the Marshall party—accompanied by Alexander's detailed map—was not acted upon until 1816. Still, its description of the James and Kanawha routes as eminently suitable and desirable had much to do with the establishment of the Virginia Board of Public Works in 1812, the first of its kind in the country. This board would take charge of road building, canal construction, river development and the creation of railroads in the Commonwealth for the next sixty years. One of its initial acts was to urge the James River Company to make good on its promise of digging a canal up to, then over, the Alleghenies.

The Commonwealth Takes Control

Getting no satisfaction, the state finally assumed control of the lethargic James River Company in 1820—and with it, the chief responsibility for inland navigation and canal construction. In return, the stockholders of the former James River Company were promised handsome dividends forever.

Even before that agreement, the Board of Public Works had been surveying the proposed western route, beginning with an 1817 report from Principal Engineer Loammi Baldwin. The following year Thomas Moore succeeded Baldwin and produced a more detailed survey, suggesting a lock-and-dam plan (known as a "slack-water navigation" system) as an alternative to the river-canal idea. Then Moore and consulting engineer Isaac Briggs mapped the route a third time.

The fourth survey of this series was done by Moore's replacement, Claudius Crozet, with Judge Benjamin Wright serving as consultant. Wright was then the chief engineer of the nearly completed Erie Canal in New York, and he joined Crozet in recommending a canal on the James with a turnpike across the Allegheny Mountains.

1820

In 1827, two years after the completion of the Erie Canal, Captain William G. McNeill of the Army Corps of Engineers reported that an all-water route over the mountains was feasible, a goal that Virginia canal advocates were to pursue vigorously for the next fifty years.

These men gained encouragement from the instant success of the Erie Canal. Stretching from Albany on the Hudson River westward to Lake Erie, a distance of 363 miles, it represented the greatest transportation improvement the young and expansive nation had ever seen, and inaugurated a great wave of canal building. Soon Pennsylvania extended its commerce over the mountains by a canal to the Ohio River, and Maryland planned a canal along the Potomac. To the west, Ohio and Indiana started carving out canal connections between the Great Lakes and the Ohio River.

There was also the growing challenge of the railroads. Just as the Erie Canal was becoming a reality, in 1825 George Stephenson completed the 125-mile Stockton and Darlington Railroad in England, his steam locomotive pulling the first successful passenger train. Soon this innovation spread to the former colonies, with the Baltimore and Ohio Railroad breaking ground on July 4, 1828—ironically, the same day as did the Chesapeake and Ohio Canal on the Potomac River. (President John Quincy Adams chose to attended the canal groundbreaking.)

During this same period the now state-owned James River Company extended the James River Canal to Maiden's Adventure Dam, twenty-eight

Claudius Crozet, principal engineer of Virginia, 1823. Crozet surveyed and pushed for the canal twenty-eight miles above Richmond and seven miles through the Blue Ridge Gorge in the 1820s.

Engineers Learn by Doing

The engineering, construction and maintenance of Virginia's canal system was no mean feat—particularly since the training of engineers in this era was largely limited to practical, on-the-job experience.

The first man to call himself a civil engineer was an Englishman, John Smeaton, in 1761. The first degree in civil engineering in this country was awarded in 1835 by the Rensselaer School at Troy, New York. Prior to this, the only American-trained engineers were West Point graduates, and only fifteen of them were working as civil engineers as late as 1830.

It was in 1816 that Claudius Crozet arrived at West Point from France to help organize the new school, and he was largely responsible for developing an engineering program. A graduate of the *Ecole Polytechnique* of Paris, he was to play a major role in the development of Virginia's early transportation systems.

While canals date back to antiquity and were helping to develop Europe in the 1600s, it was not until about the mid-1700s that England first started its canal system and not until the late 1700s that any work was started in this country. Except for one or two European engineers such as William Weston in New York State, practical engineers in America were all untrained in such work. In addition, the surveying instruments and levels so necessary for determining grades and elevations were not developed in their present forms until the 1700s. Even the chain for measuring distances was not used until the 1600s, and the steel tape as we know it was first used about 1820.

miles above Richmond, and built a seven-mile Blue Ridge Canal through the rocky and treacherous Blue Ridge Gorge, parallel to the Blue Ridge Turnpike, which crossed the mountains. The Virginians also completed the 200-mile James River and Kanawha Turnpike from Covington across the Alleghenies to Charleston and on to the Big Sandy River, which flows into the Ohio near present-day Huntington, West Virginia.

All this activity prompted Claudius Crozet, the state engineer, to embark on yet another survey, again assisted by Judge Wright. This time, though, the two men parted company. Crozet had become convinced that a railroad over the mountains was the answer, while Wright remained loyal to the canal. In 1830 they filed separate and conflicting reports to a General Assembly still dominated by the canal interests. One man in particular, House Delegate Joseph C. Cabell, was furious with Crozet. Even though many agreed with the engineer's report, Cabell convinced his colleagues to cut Crozet's pay in half for 1831. Not surprisingly, Crozet quit. Decades later, in his 1886 report on the condition of Virginia (and its canals) after the Civil War, former Confederate General John D. Imboden referred to the Crozet/Cabell disagreement by noting: "Crozet found a lion in his path."

Canal Note
The canal was stressed financially almost from the start.
NOTE COURTESY CLIFTON W. POTTER

1830

Joseph Carrington Cabell, first president of the James River and Kanawha Company
COURTESY RANDY CABELL

Cabell Creates the James River and Kanawha Company

Whatever the plan, it had become obvious by 1832 that the state-owned James River Company was not going to be able to carry it out. Joseph C. Cabell, a brilliant and able legislator and longtime advocate of the canal extension, led an effort that resulted in a charter being granted for a joint stock company called the James River and Kanawha Company. It permitted either a combination of canal (Richmond to Lynchburg or above) and a railroad over the mountains to the Kanawha, or a railway over the entire distance.

1835

It was not until 1835 that Cabell, with the able assistance of Chief Justice Marshall, was able to raise the $4 million in stock subscriptions required by the canal charter. Of this the state paid $2 million, plus credit of another million to represent the value of the old canal properties. Private investors subscribed less than $1 million, with Richmond, Lynchburg, and the banks making up the balance. At the stockholders meeting on May 25, 1835, Cabell was elected president, and the stockholders chose to build a canal to Covington and a railroad across the mountains. Crozet's plan had triumphed over Wright's, at least for the moment.

The day after the James River and Kanawha Company's organizational stockholders meeting ended on May 28, 1835, the new board of directors—or "The Directory," as Cabell liked to call them—gathered for the first time. Organizing a corps of engineers was one of the principal orders of business.

At the meeting in December of 1835, President Cabell, noting the stockholders' concern that the first contracts for construction be let by early winter, reported: "The President and Directors, therefore decided to organize a corps of engineers with all practicable despatch, in order to press the line with vigor during the intermediate time."

Judge Benjamin Wright, first chief engineer of the canal. Wright had been chief engineer of the Erie Canal, completed in 1825. He consulted on many canals, including the James River in 1824–25 and 1830. He and Crozet did not agree on many points.

Engineer's drawing of Byrd Creek aqueduct above Richmond. See photos on pages 144–145.

Judge Wright Accepts the Challenge

The public voice, Cabell argued, clearly favored Judge Benjamin Wriqht, Esq., of New York, as the fit agent to conduct the work of building the canal. Cabell gave Wright high praise: "For his acknowledged talents, his long experience, his eminent success, and his unsullied integrity, he had been recognized as the head of the practical engineers of the United States and possessed in a peculiar degree the confidence of the people of this state."

The James River and Kanawha Company board drafted a letter to Judge Wright offering him the job. He sent back a prompt affirmative reply. The

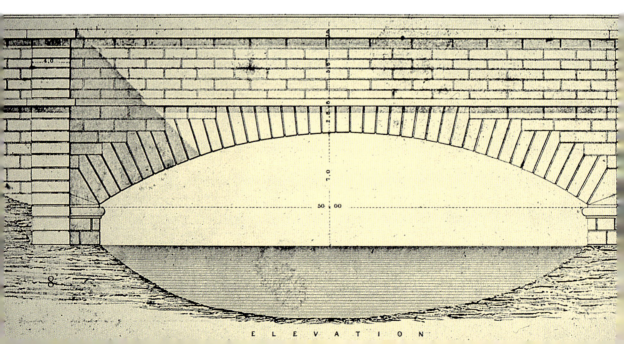

ELEVATION

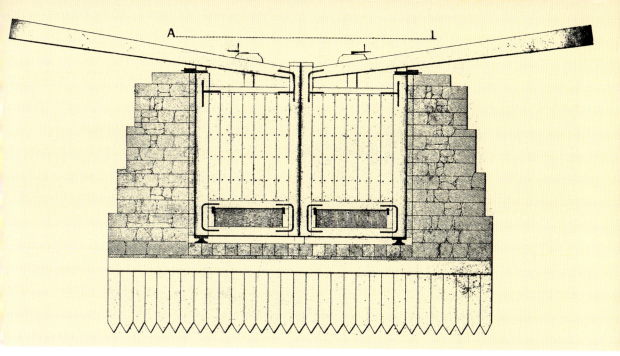

Lock Gate detail for the JR&K Canal from a drawing by Benjamin Wright

judge was, indeed, a logical choice, though probably not as universally popular as Cabell indicated. As a young man in upper New York State, Wright had done some land surveying. In 1794 he assisted William Weston, a noted English canal engineer, on surveys for what later became a part of the Erie Canal. He was a member of the New York state assembly for several terms and was made a judge during the War of 1812.

When work on the Erie Canal began in 1817, Wright was the senior of three self-trained engineers selected for the project and soon became the chief engineer. By 1837 the new canal had exceeded all expectations in terms of traffic, tolls had more than repaid its initial cost, and it was already being enlarged. Even before its completion, Wright's reputation was made—and it was that reputation that prompted Virginia to hire him on two occasions as a consultant on canal surveys with Claudius Crozet.

Wright came to Virginia in June of 1835 to meet with the company's board of directors. Because of previous commitments, he told them, he could spare little time before the end of the year, but by 1836 he would be available for two-thirds or three-quarters of the time. Wright asked to be allowed to select his own assistants and draw on them for his field work, and Cabell reported that the judge "would be willing to risk his reputation upon the result." The board agreed to these terms, ignoring provisions in its charter requiring that the chief engineer reside in the state. Wright, born in 1770, was almost sixty-five years old at the time.

Wright's salary was set at $3,000 for the balance of 1835 and either $5,500 or $6,000 for succeeding years, depending on how much of his time he would spend on the Virginia project. This rather handsome compensation reflected both the stature of the man and the demand for engineers on the many canals and railroads then under construction. It was even more notable in that Cabell only received $3,000 per year as president of the company.

Stovall Creek aqueduct at Galt's Mill in Amherst County illustrates the beauty and durability of canal construction. Note the coping stones at the top and the line of stones below forming the bottom of the waterway. The middle pier supports two twenty-four-foot arches. See also page 121.

After agreeing to serve on his own terms, Judge Wright named his son Simon W. Wright as one of his assistant engineers. The others were Daniel Livermore and Charles Ellet, Jr., both from Pennsylvania. Each of the three was to receive $2,000 per year. Wright and Cabell then appointed fifteen surveyors and the needed rodmen and chainmen. Fourteen of the surveying appointments, according to Cabell, "were conferred upon natives of the state, the greater part entering the corps with the view of adopting the business of civil engineering as a profession for life."

A plan of action was approved at the next meeting: the decision was made to extend the canal from Richmond to Covington, provide a railroad over the mountains to the Great Falls of the Kanawha River, and improve the Kanawha for steamboat travel from there to the Ohio River at Point Pleasant. The canal on the James River was to be divided into three parts, or divisions: the first from Richmond to Lynchburg, the second from Lynchburg to Pattonsburg (on the north side of the river across from Buchanan), and the third from Pattonsburg to Covington.

At that point, stock subscriptions were less than 40 percent of the $4 million projected cost, so the Virginia Bureau of Public Works made an exception to its own rules by allocating 60 percent instead of the usual 40 percent to the canal project.

The Great Work Begins

Work on the "First Grand Division," as Cabell called it, was to be under contract by December of 1835, with completion scheduled for 1838. In order to accomplish this, Wright divided the work of the first division into three sections, with an assistant engineer in charge of each. After giving directions, he left for the North.

The first section began at the end of the old works at Maiden's Adventure Dam, twenty-eight miles above Richmond, and extended to Scottsville. This was put in the charge of his son Simon Wright. (The old lower canal from Maiden's Adventure to Richmond was to be rebuilt after the other work was underway.) The second section, from Scottsville to the mouth of the Tye River, would be under the direction of Daniel Livermore, another engineer who had previously worked under Wright. The final section into Lynchburg was delegated to Charles Ellet, Jr., who made the city his headquarters.

By the latter part of July the three newly formed engineering parties had assembled in Richmond. In covered boats, they moved up the river to start at the head of their respective divisions, then moved downriver to determine the best canal route.

"During the months of August and September," in Cabell's words, "the location was pressed with a degree of energy and zeal deserving the highest praise."

Theirs was a tremendous undertaking. The engineers had to make initial surveys to locate the best route for the canal, determine elevations and grades, pinpoint where to place the locks, and create the maps that the assessors needed to condemn the right of way. Plans, specifications, and contracts had to be drawn up and copied, not only for the canal proper, but for all the complementary structures such as dams, locks, culverts, aqueducts, and bridges.

In October Judge Wright returned to tour the line and review the plans. His report of October 6 approved seventy-three miles to be let to bids and forty-seven miles to be examined further.

The magnitude of the work required of the engineers on this first segment soon caused a further division of authority in the engineering corps. In November, the three assistant engineers were made "principal assistant engineers" and their sections renamed "principal divisions." These three divisions were divided further into sub-sections supervised by "assistant engineers."

Cabell asked Charles Ellet to visit the Chesapeake and Ohio Canal and find agents who could locate quarries and hydraulic cement. Judge Charles Kinsey, who had been associated with the Morris Canal in New Jersey, was appointed to perform a similar function.

Bids were let, totaling over $586,000, mainly for the excavation of the canal sections, and approved on December 10, 1835. Bids for the stone structures were deferred until spring to ascertain the resources of the country for stone and waterproof lime, according to Cabell. It was more probable that plans were not yet complete nor locations accurately determined.

Specifications for the canal channel called for it to be at least fifty feet wide at the water surface, thirty feet wide at the bottom, and five feet deep. The banks on each side were to be sloped to rise one foot in two, with the tops two feet higher than the water. The towpath on the river side would be at least twelve feet wide, the opposite, or "berm" bank, at least eight feet wide. Both were to slope slightly away from the canal for drainage.

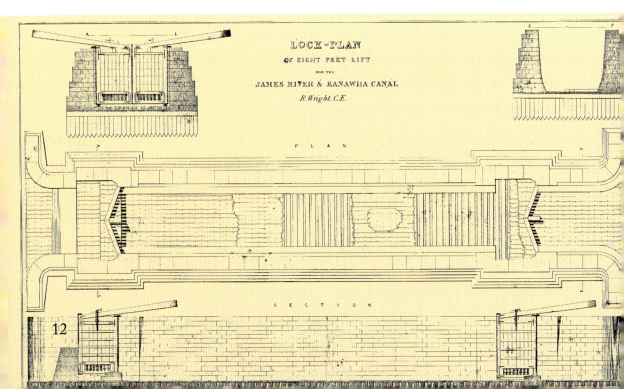

This lock plan for the JR&K Canal is signed R. Wright, C.E.

Workers excavate a canal channel using two-wheeled carts drawn by mules.
COURTESY CANAL SQUARE AT SCOTTSVILLE, VA

The first work on the line was backbreaking, beginning with grubbing and clearing for the whole width required. All trees and bushes were cut back to the ground for at least twenty feet on each side of the proposed channel.

Heavy embankments were then formed, using two-wheeled carts drawn by horses, oxen, or mules to haul the dirt. These were built up in successive layers not more than six inches deep. Lighter embankments, where wheelbarrows could be used, were built up in layers not more than one foot deep. The portions of the canal's interior where the soil appeared porous was "puddled" with clay of suitable thickness, wetted to obtain a proper consistency, and properly tamped.

Towpath banks exposed to erosion by the river were walled with solid or broken rip-rap stone. It was part of the responsibility of the engineers to balance the cuts and fills as nearly as possible.

No spiritous liquor was allowed. Laborers were subject to dismissal for bad workmanship, intemperance, or disorderly conduct.

Shocked Property Owners

The canal company's burst of activity soon alarmed some landowners along the route. Their best bottom lands were in danger of being cut in two, and they were downright unhappy with the financial compensation they were offered. Cabell failed to grasp their objections. As far as he could see, any injuries caused by the canal were largely offset by its benefits.

Two of the more prominent among the discontented were Judge John Robertson (who had acquired the large Mount Athos Plantation, near Lynchburg, at the death of Colonel William S. Lewis in 1828) and his cousin, Colonel William Bolling of Bolling Hall in Goochland County. Both men were also stockholders.

Not only was Judge Robertson a congressman, but his brother Wyndham would become governor of Virginia in 1836. In December 1835, John Robertson said he would hold the James River & Kanawha Company responsible for trespassing if its workers disturbed the garden of his miller on Archer Creek. In January 1836, he wrote that the company and contractor would also be held responsible for any unlawful entry. Later that month he accused the

1836

Charles Ellet, Jr.

Born in Pennsylvania in 1810, Charles Ellet, Jr. was just twenty-six years old when elevated to the responsible position of chief engineer. Despite his youth and relative lack of formal education, he displayed a talent for mathematics and languages and proved a capable engineer. He had also demonstrated considerable initiative and dedication ever since starting work in 1827 with a survey party on one of the Pennsylvania canals.

The Chesapeake and Ohio Canal on the north bank of the Potomac River was just being organized in 1828, with Judge Wright as chief engineer, when Ellet applied for a job as a voluntary assistant. He remained for two years. Hindered by his youth and anxious for more training, he then left for France. The French Revolution interrupted his studies at the polytechnical school, so he toured France, Switzerland, and England, observing and sketching canals, bridges, and railroads.

Upon arriving back home in 1832, rather than returning to his old position, Ellet turned his attention to bridge building. When his initial plan for a span across the Potomac at Washington was not accepted, he took a job with a New York railroad in 1833. The next year, he again went to work under Judge Wright, this time on the New York and Erie Railroad.

Wright was sufficiently impressed with his protege's industry and promised to bring him along to Virginia for the James River and Kanawha project, and Joseph Cabell asked Ellet to use his Chesapeake and Ohio contacts to find agents to locate quarries and hydraulic cement. Cabell also sent Ellet to New York at one point to secure surveying instruments.

Still, the brash young man's appointment as chief engineer on the James River was not made without some reservations on the part of the board. After the appointment, board secretary W. B. Chittenden wrote the new chief: "To be perfectly frank, there have been expressions of yours in your intercourse with the Board of Directors . . . to be construed as dictatorial, if not sarcastic. . . ."

By January of 1837, Ellet was complaining that his salary was too low for a chief engineer. This resulted in a raise to $5,000, which he supplemented with outside consulting work. Ellet lived in Lynchburg, where he had moved to take charge of the second canal section. He apparently liked it there, and joined one of the city's most prominent families with his October 31, 1837, marriage to Elvira "Ellie" Daniel, daughter of Judge William Daniel, Sr.

While in Lynchburg the couple lived at Point of Honor, Elvira's family home. This restored Lynchburg landmark still stands overlooking the remains of the canal below.

At the time of Ellet's wedding, the local newspaper referred to him as "Principle Engineer of the James River and Kanawha Company," and his union with Elvira proved successful and happy despite his occasionally prickly temperament. The same, however, cannot be said of his relationship with the board. Ellet was fired in 1839.

He would make a lasting name for himself by designing and constructing the first wire-suspension bridge in America, spanning the Schuylkill River at Philadelphia, in 1842. Another at Niagara Falls in 1848 featured some theatrics: Ellet held a contest paying five dollars to the first to fly a kite across the river, and later he made an astounding charioteer-like drive over his just-laid catwalk. The Niagara project ended badly for Ellet who began collecting tolls for the bridge without permission from the bridge directors. A court order forced Ellet and his family to leave town, and eventually his rival John Roebling completed the railroad and vehicular bridge. In 1849 Ellet went on to build the then-longest suspension bridge in the world, over the Ohio River at Wheeling, West Virginia (which Roebling soon surpassed).

During the Civil War he commanded a steam ram fleet of his own design in the Battle of Memphis, successfully ramming all but one Confederate ram ship on the Mississippi. Shot in the knee during the battle, Ellett died from his wound (complicated by the measles which he contracted in the hospital) two weeks later. After rushing in a vain attempt to meet him in Cairo, Missouri, Elvira died from exhaustion and a broken heart the day after the funeral.

company of acting solely in its own interest and completely disregarding his in locating the canal so close to his Fredonian Mill. (The stonework of this mill is still standing on Archer Creek.)

As might be expected, Joseph Cabell proved a hard man to intimidate. The next month Robertson wrote brother Wyndham that while his admonitions had stopped the canal company's line through the miller's garden, they then threatened to plow through the center of his lowgrounds instead—for spite, he presumed, as punishment for daring to defend his rights. Yet he had no fear that he could arrest this move also, or "make them smoke for damages." Finally, in December 1836, Cabell reported that Judge Robertson's legal objections were settled by a compromise.

The engineers often dined at the home of Colonel Bolling and spent the night there, but he complained privately and bitterly in his diary about the canal project. In August of 1836, he wrote that Cabell and some of the directors had viewed the line, but had not decided between two alternatives. Bolling suspected, he confided to his journal, that they had decided on the one doing him the most damage—this, in order to save a few thousand dollars at his expense. He believed that they totally disregarded the interest of the land proprietors. Yet on one occasion, when the officials stayed overnight and Cabell became ill, Bolling sent him back home in his own carriage.

On August 23, 1836, Bolling attended the directors' meeting to find his suspicions well-founded. Outraged, he noted his belief that the directors had no opinions of their own and so were of no use; that the advice of their "Yankee engineers" was "Law and Gospel" to them, and they were perfectly reckless in the injuries they inflicted on individuals. He also noted that his cousin John Robertson was present, and that he too had found the directors immovable.

The assessors reviewed the Bolling Hall land again on October 31, with the colonel insisting that anything less than $15,000 was short of what he ought in justice to receive. In December he was awarded $7,600 for about seventy acres of land, most of it he noted among the most valuable he owned. He had made $100 worth of tobacco per acre on this land that year, he grumbled, "without one particle of manure."

After finally accepting the $7,600 in January 1837, Bolling said if he were twenty years younger, he would have risked loss of the whole damages to oppose the company's decision. On February 10, he took what he had received from that "iniquitous corporation, the James River & Kanawha Company" and invested it. He also sold his stock in the company for $75 per share to one of the other directors. This represented a loss of $25 per share, but turned out to be astute, as the stock's value continued to decline.

Another who stood up to the company was John Percival, who lived just downstream from Lynchburg. In 1838, with the canal nearly completed to that city, the company found itself at an impasse. When the contractor attempted to start work, he was stopped by Mr. Percival, "threatening certain and immediate death to any agent of the company who should enter his lands for the purpose

In foreground, the waterworks dam of Lynchburg. In 1835 the company contracted with the city to maintain the dam and assure the city of an adequate water supply. Scott's Mill Dam and Scott's Mill shown beyond it were added later. The structure between the dams is a fish ladder to allow shad to pass and spawn, as required by state ordinance.

of excavating the canal." Percival was demanding five times the amount allowed by the assessors for his land, and it took a special act of the General Assembly in March 1840 to settle the dispute in favor of the company.

Ellet Requests More Engineers

When the three assistant engineers submitted written reports to the board at the end of the first year, Simon Wright and Daniel Livermore both closed by expressing appreciation for the kindness and hospitality of the landowners along the line. Livermore went so far as to say he felt that a friendly feeling toward the enterprise was generally manifested, in spite of the inconvenience it sometimes caused. Ellet, who had crossed Judge Robertson, had no comment. This proved to be typical of his relations with both property owners and canal administration.

Charles Ellet, Jr., was undoubtedly the most able, experienced, and energetic of the three principal assistant engineers. Evidently it was he who had made the request to the board asking for more engineers to expedite the project, and they agreed to increase the staff.

In a November 1835 letter, Ellet explained in more detail why he felt additional skilled help was needed. After the initial location of the line, he wrote, these extra engineers would be kept busy "superintending the construction of the work, giving the contractors the necessary marks for sloping the banks and building their walls, marking out the locks and culverts, measuring and inspecting the materials, preparing the monthly estimates, and drawing the plans of the detail of every part of every structure." By 1837 there were assistants to the engineers on the line.

As it turned out, Judge Wright's leadership of the James River & Kanawha Canal project was brief. On February 20, 1836, he submitted his resignation, citing advancing age and bodily infirmity. He may also have tired of complaints from Virginians that he was not a resident of their state, for he resurfaced the same year as chief engineer on the Tioga and Chemung Railroad in upstate New York.

Wright did indicate a desire to continue his association with the Virginia company as a consultant, however, making quarterly visits to the work. He further recommended Ellet as his replacement. The board agreed to retain Wright in this new capacity at his regular salary of $5,000, and Ellet was made chief engineer on March 24 at a salary of $3,000.

Miffed at being passed over for a junior colleague (and by his father, no less), Simon Wright promptly resigned. A few months later Daniel Livermore also left the project—from "indisposition," as Cabell put it. Colonel Bolling, in his diary for May 22, 1836, explained it better. He noted meeting "Messrs. Ellet and Livermore, engineers on the James River and Kanawha Canal, the latter deranged and of course must be displaced [sic]."

In order to start the task of enlarging the old canal above Richmond, the board agreed to hire four "principal assistant engineers" under Ellet. However, the great demand for engineers throughout the country made it possible to find only three qualified assistants at that time.

View from the canal towpath of Locher Cement Plant at Blue Ridge Dam. The original plant was rebuilt about 1850. All of the cement used on the canal and later on the railroads was made there.

To get the work on the canal moving, Ellet divided the 120 miles of line from just east of Richmond to Lynchburg into 201 sections, each to be bid separately. While these plans were progressing, Cabell sent Ellet to travel the Pennsylvania Canal for its full distance from Philadelphia to Pittsburgh.

Early in 1836 Charles Kinsey—the board's advisor from New Jersey—had located a good supply of bluish limestone rock suitable for hydraulic cement on the James in Bedford County, across the river from what is now Glasgow. Arrangements were made with Nelson Tinsley to quarry and burn the stone and grind it into cement, but more expensive cement still had to be imported from New York until Tinsley's operation could begin in earnest in 1840.

To supply the canal with water, one of the company's first acts in 1835 had been to contract with the town of Lynchburg to take control of its waterworks dam. This municipal waterworks, one of the earliest in the country, had been completed in 1830. In return, the company agreed to maintain the dam and canal and to assure Lynchburg of an adequate water supply.

Work had hardly begun on this aspect of the project, however, when a great freshet, as floods were called ("The highest that has taken place for the last half century," according to Cabell), damaged the Lynchburg dam severely in June 1836. This required immediate rebuilding under the superintendence of the chief engineer, who directed the water-supply canal to be moved to higher ground. And none too soon, for an even-higher flood in late August destroyed most of the old canal.

In his characteristically optimistic report to the stockholders, Cabell congratulated the engineers on their clairvoyance and observed: "Two such floods in the same year, constitutes a combination of events of very extraordinary and remarkable character." He added that since the dam was an insufficient structure and would have had to be rebuilt anyway, the loss was not a great one.

In January 1837 the board hired William Lake, a capable English engineer, as a principal assistant to direct the rebuilding of the twenty-eight miles of the original canal between Maiden's Adventure and Richmond. (This move at least found favor with Colonel Bolling, who considered Lake more congenial than the previous "Yankee" engineers). Lake's first task was to survey this section and develop a plan for rebuilding that would include an enlarged water supply into the Richmond basin.

Municipal leaders in Virginia's capital already envisioned a great influx of trade and commerce upon the completion of its connection to the west, enough to annoint Richmond a major eastern city. Taking that cue, Cabell noted that of the surplus water available, there was not only enough "to supply the present mills and manufactories, but enough to meet a great and growing demand for ages to come." The engineers ruled the water supply to be adequate and estimated that enough space was available to erect the "100 respectable establishments" Cabell felt would certainly be ultimately required.

Cement mine surface openings are still present at Balcony Falls. The twelve-foot-thick vein of dark bluish limestone lies on a 30°–40° slope. Natural cement was made from certain rock with a composition that was less uniform than, but similar to, present Portland cement, which has replaced it.

Lock 46 is a good example of a composite lock. This is a wooden lock with rough stone walls originally lined with timber and planking. Note the timber post at right and horizontal slots for 4" timber bolted in place. Photo was taken after excavation by Gibson Hobbs and his friends.

On a wider scale, though, the national economic picture did not encourage such undertakings. A financial panic that developed in 1837 made labor cheaper and more available, but it also brought financial problems for the company. Assessments on the stockholders were slow in coming in, and the company was undercapitalized. All this made more cost-cutting measures necessary.

Therefore, after much study, Chief Engineer Ellet proposed that the planned expensive cut-stone locks be changed to wood, or composite locks of stone and wood. These would be built with rough stone side-walls lined with heavy wood planking and with wooden bottoms to make them watertight. Of the fifty-one locks, twenty-nine had not yet been contracted, mostly because of the shortage of good stone and trained masons. Ellet calculated the cost of a wooden lock at $3,000 each, versus $11,800 each for locks built entirely of stone, or a total savings of $232,000. He argued that the interest on the savings would more than pay for the additional maintenance. By extending his calculations to the locks from Lynchburg to Covington, he figured a total savings of $960,000.

Not only would this facilitate the opening of the lower sections of the canal much sooner, thereby gaining added revenue, but it would also permit the use of those sections to haul good stone and supplies to the upper works at lower cost. Such a system would still allow replacement of the temporary locks with permanent stone locks at a later date, and the wooden locks would be located so as to make it easy to build the stone locks adjoining. By this and other reasoning, Ellet concluded that the permanent stone locks later would cost only $370 more than if installed when first planned.

Wright, as consulting engineer, agreed. He further recommended that a model of such a lock be built on the scale of one inch to the foot, representing every piece of timber used and how it was to be put together so the contractors would know exactly what was expected. A reading of the lengthy and complicated specifications for these locks indicates this was a good idea, but the record gives no hint of whether any of the models were actually made.

The recesses for the gates of these locks and the entrances to the gates were of dressed stone, as in the original plan. But the numerous rough-stone inner walls, still visible along the canal line today, clearly show that the ambitious goal of replacing the wooden locks was never accomplished. The heavy iron bolts protruding from the rough stone walls are the only indication today of the fine oak and heart pine timber linings. With no water in the canal, timbers left exposed to the elements have long since decayed.

Expansive Plans

Despite the faltering economy Ellet continued to emphasize the big picture. In August 1837, in the conclusion of his report on the proposed railroad route from Covington to the Great Falls of the Kanawha, he once again invoked the shining example of the Erie Canal. After ten years of operation, he pointed out, New York State was receiving nearly $1,300,000 in tolls annually from its inland waterway, which each year carried 100,000 people westward. In 1834, Ellet added, the Pennsylvania Canal from Philadelphia to Pittsburgh was hauling a vast tonnage.

Ellet justified the cost and effort of completing a line to the Ohio in these words: "The improvement creates the trade, and the trade which it creates supports the work that brought it into existence."

Despite his heavy workload with the James River & Kanawha Company, the chief engineer found time to write and publish a number of reports and studies on trade, tolls, and the like. In reference to one of these, he wrote that it was "a work that was written piecemeal in almost every tavern on the canal line between Richmond and the Ohio, and in a manuscript that was sent from [my] saddlebags to the press."

By the end of 1837, the James River and Kanawha Canal was well on its way to completion as far as Lynchburg. In his report to the stockholders, President Cabell noted:

> The Construction of the new canal from Maiden's Adventure to Lynchburg has advanced with steadiness and energy throughout the present year; and the valley of the river has exhibited a vast scene of activity and animation—the assistant engineers and their parties passing on their daily rounds, the principal assistants moving in their more extended circles, the chief engineer performing his monthly tours, the consulting engineer making his quarterly visits, the contractors and their throngs of laborers and teams forming a line almost unbroken of the most lively and cheering industry for 120 miles….

1838

The total force employed on the new improvements, in December last, amounted to about 1,400 men. It rose in January to about 2,500; from which it advanced in April to about 3,500. It is at this time about 3,300, and will probably be considerably augmented soon after the public letting [of contracts] on the 14th of the month.

Thus did the president proudly report on the progress made, speaking to the stockholders at their third annual meeting in December of that year in Richmond.

True, the First Grand Division was not finished by 1838 as the board had hoped, but with much work underway they felt confident it would be completed by the following year. Moreover, although finances were strained, the board considered Ellet's reports and thought it desirable to start construction on the Second Division from Lynchburg to Buchanan. Some work was let in September, and more surveys were conducted for the water line to Covington, and for the railroad from Covington to the Kanawha River.

Edward H. Gill, an engineer with experience on several canals—the last being on the Sandy and Beaver in Ohio—was hired as principal assistant engineer to head up this work, along with two assistants. For the route over the mountains they drew heavily upon the 1827 survey of the Army Corps of Engineers prepared by Captain William G. McNeill. Charles Ellet collaborated in these later surveys, findings, and recommendations.

Ellet's report on the canal to Covington included a listing of the dams, locks, tunnels, and other structures he felt were needed. It also included, in great detail, a design plan for the mountain railroad, which included a two-and-one-half-mile tunnel through the Allegheny Mountains near White Sulphur Springs and two smaller tunnels. The chief engineer felt strongly that where distance, and thereby time of travel, could be saved, the extra expense of these was justified. This was at a time when hand drills and black powder were the only tools, and no such tunnel had ever been completed in this country.

Joseph Cabell, however, continued to cling to his dream of an unbroken water route from Richmond to the Ohio. At the meeting of December 1838, he persuaded the board to consider this plan again, and they adopted a resolution calling for another survey of the route based on a canal over the mountains.

No Reward for Engineer Ellet

By this time Chief Engineer Ellet had done most of the canal planning, nearly all of the First Division was under contract, and the Second Division to Buchanan was underway. From reading the record it appears no man could have worked harder or more faithfully. Ellet was deeply convinced of the need for the waterway and dedicated to its completion.

Unfortunately, it had also become obvious that there was not room within the same company for the strong opinions of both Ellet and Cabell. As with Crozet, a personality conflict developed and festered, and Cabell finally arranged for Ellet not to be reappointed as chief engineer at the beginning of 1839. He also chose not to inform Ellet of this immediately, leaving the unsuspecting chief toiling in the same capacity, with the same salary, until he was unceremoniously replaced by Judge Wright in May. Wright, now nearly sixty-nine, agreed to live in Virginia full time, and his old job of consulting engineer was eliminated.

Ellet was shocked and complained bitterly. He undoubtedly had done a fine job, but his independent manner contributed to his downfall. Even his wife, Ellie, once pointed this out in a letter, noting

> Many think you erred in not showing Mr. Cabell sufficient respect, and in making him appear of too little consequence. They say your temper is too dictatorial. Everyone gives you credit for talent of the highest order, but many think your disposition overbearing in the extreme . . . expressing a belief that you have been far too dictatorial, and assumed more authority than rightly fell to you.

Rather harsh words from a devoted wife.

Predictably, Ellet did not go quietly, bringing suit against the company in 1840 for the balance of his pay in 1839. This was not settled until 1843. Ellet, paying the court expenses of the defendant, lost his case.

Cabell was highly pleased to have Judge Wright back as the chief engineer. In his annual report for 1839, he said in part, "the management of the work by this gentleman has been as skillful and efficient as his personal conduct and deportment have been amiable and acceptable in all his relations; as well to the President and Directors of the company, as to the engineering corps, the body of contractors and the proprietors of the line."

Colonel Bolling apparently did not share these sentiments. In his diary for November 27, 1837, he wrote: "Judge Wright, engineer of the canal, and a demi-god with Cabell, the President . . . came (with others) uninvited and staid [sic] all night."

In dry summers, when the timbers of the two wooden dams of the old canal shrank and leaked so badly they could not fill the canal, Bolling's diary also expressed his disgust at the engineers and officers for their incompetence. Still, he was greatly pleased when in 1837 he rode over "to see Mr. Lipper, the draughtsman [sic] of the company, who had undertaken and commenced an elegant map of my estate at this place."

By the end of 1839, with much of the work on the First Division nearing completion, the engineering staff was reduced. However, most of the contracts for the works above Lynchburg to the North (now Maury) River were let in November, partly to preserve at least some of the engineering staff. This action, done in spite of severe financial problems, was to bring considerable criticism from both stockholders and the public.

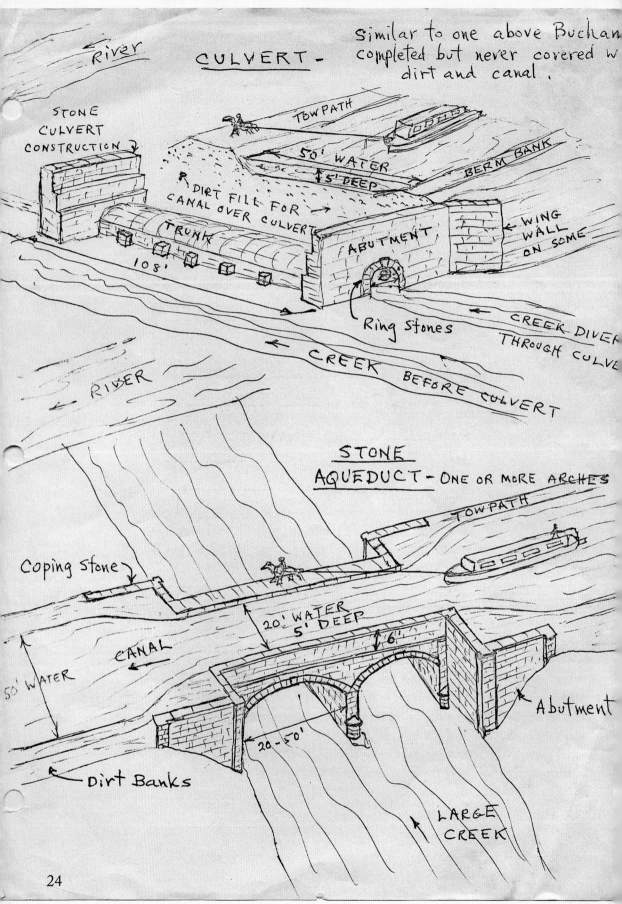

The First Grand Division

In 1839 Cabell gave a comprehensive annual report that included a complete description of the whole line from Richmond to Lynchburg. Taken from his observations and the reports of the engineers, it is the best available record of each level, with each of the many locks, dams, culverts, aqueducts, farm bridges and the like enumerated. He also noted the mills, iron furnaces and other establishments that he saw as possible sources of revenue along the canal.

The 146½ miles of canal were divided into fifty-one levels, each separated by a lock to raise or lower the boats. The average lift was over eight feet, and with fifty-one locks, this gave a total rise in elevation of almost 428 feet between Richmond and Lynchburg.

The canal followed the river on the north side from Richmond all the way upstream into Amherst County. There, it crossed over to the south side into Campbell County at the lower end of Judge Robertson's Mount Athos Plantation, below Lynchburg. A rope ferry was used to pull the boats across the river, using early Roebling* wire rope cables. The ferry was a substitute for an earlier towpath bridge that was badly damaged by ice before completion. The canal then stayed on the south side of the river into Lynchburg.

The canal was located away from the river when possible, and on a level high enough to be above all but the highest flood waters. Given this elevation, and in order to control the water in the canal, the natural streams along the route had to pass under the man-made waterway.

Dismantling the wooden crib dam at Coleman's Falls above Lynchburg. During drought conditions the timbers of the dam would dry out and shrink, causing the dam to leak so that it could not fill the canal. Note the stone fill for stability. A stone dam for power generation now replaces it.

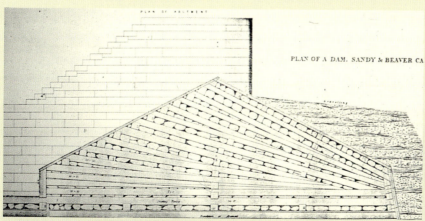

Drawing of a typical wood dam cross section without the plank covering, Sandy & Beaver Canal

Construction was finished on this culvert five miles above Buchanan, but the stone arch was never covered with earth. See other photos on page 101.

*German-born and -educated engineer John Roebling began his career surveying and building canals and railroads in Pennsylvania. At the time, canal boats were placed on railroad cars and pulled by nine-inch-thick hemp rope up inclines over the Allegheny Mountains. One day while he was watching, the rope snapped, sending a boat to the bottom of the mountain. He remembered a German engineering paper about wire rope and soon began developing his own rope-making technique. Roebling sold his first cable in 1841 and began developing it for use in suspension bridges. He designed and built a suspension aqueduct over the Allegheny River, a suspension bridge over the Monongahela at Pittsburgh, and several others, before finishing what Charles Ellet had started on the Niagara River, building a two-level bridge for vehicles and trains. He died from an on-the-job injury he received while undertaking his most famous project, the Brooklyn Bridge, completed by his son Washington.

Alfred Brown Peticolas 1859 sketch of excavation of a railroad cut in Amherst County near Lynchburg. The same techniques were used in canal work.
COURTESY VIRGINIA HISTORICAL SOCIETY

Note the holes drilled for wedging to split the stone were closer than necessary on this coping stone at Lock 46.

With smaller creeks, this was accomplished by arched stone culverts more than 100 feet long and of sufficient width to carry the water of the streams. On top of the culverts rested the full width of the dirt canal channel, the towpath and the berm bank for two-way traffic. For larger streams, aqueducts were built, sometimes with several arched spans over the stream. These carried wooden or stone waterways twenty feet wide to allow for one boat at a time to pass. A total of 191 culverts, eleven aqueducts, and 133 farm bridges over the canal were built on the First Division, along with the necessary locks and lockkeepers' houses. The company found that the wooden farm bridges, in particular, required much maintenance.

By contrast, the arched stone culverts and aqueducts were referred to as "works of art," and a great number are still intact. Instead of canal boats, however, they now carry long, heavy coal trains that rumble across them without causing any signs of stress. They are truly beautiful examples of the master stonemason's work.

Five dams were used to feed the First Division of the canal, two of them—Bosher's Dam and the Maiden's Adventure Dam—were left over from the old James River Company canal. These wooden crib structures were filled with stone, as were the two new dams at Tye River and Joshua Falls. The rebuilt waterworks dam at Lynchburg was a curved stone structure that still stands.

A guard lock at each dam was built at a level that normally allowed boats to pass through to the pond without being lifted. These devices were also used to control the flow of water to the canal below. The headwalls (abutments) of the dams were elevated so floodwaters would not spill over from the ponds into the canal below.

Boats moved through the ponds created by these dams, and the towpath followed the bank to the head of the ponds. Here, "outlet locks" lifted the boats from the ponds back up into the canal. Travel on these ponds was called "slackwater navigation."

Earth Moving and Stone Work

The stretch of canal from Richmond to Lynchburg took nearly five years to complete. Company records show that the work consisted of nearly 8,500,000 cubic yards of earth excavation and over 210,000 cubic yards of stone-walling and riprap. All of this was accomplished with tools that today would seem primitive—manpower, picks and shovels, hand drills, black powder, crude wooden derricks, horse carts, and boats.

The stone work was the most difficult of all. Slabs were cut from the quarries by hand drilling and splitting. To split hard stone, holes about four inches deep and four to eight inches apart were drilled along the split line. Tapered iron wedges followed, driven into all the holes until the stone split. The finish dressing was done by hand with small chisels and hammers.

The stones lining the locks were hammer-dressed to make them smooth enough not to abrade the sides of the boats. Equally smooth were those placed in the keystone arches of the culverts and aqueducts. Since many of the larger stones weighed three to five tons, wooden, jib-type derricks with rope and block were needed to hoist them into place.

Canal Workers

Labor was a particular concern of the engineers. Contractors, many of whom were property owners using their own slaves or other local help, had to be screened and carefully supervised after construction had started.

This was not so much a problem where the earthwork was concerned, but the more critical and time-consuming stonework was often delayed for want of good masons and stone of good quality along some stretches of the river.

Irish canal workers
COURTESY SCOTTSVILLE CANAL SQUARE

The engineers had hoped to let bids for most of the masonry contracts by August of 1836, only to find that canal and railroad construction in the North had absorbed many trained men and skilled immigrant labor. Other potential James River canal workers were discouraged by reports of unhealthy working conditions, especially in swampy areas (Irishmen, it was said, were particularly leery of snakes). Many contractors depended on slave labor, but some landowners were reluctant to send their slaves for hire because they feared poor treatment.

To offset this domestic labor shortage, the board sent an agent to Scotland that same August to recruit stone masons. The company planned to pay for their passage, and then offer moderate wages both until the advances were repaid, and until one year thereafter. They hoped to recruit up to 400 masons, but got only thirty-two. In the same year an agent was sent to Germany to hire up to 1,000 mechanics and common laborers, but he got only 346.

By the winter of 1836-37, however, help became more plentiful. As Cabell noted, "a great number of companies at the north and west having, from pecuniary difficulties of the times, suspended their operations, labour to a large amount, both mechanical and common, was thrown loose upon the market." With that influx, orders to overseas agents were canceled. Even so, by late 1837 the thirty-two

Gravestone in Snowden of a child of a canal worker. A number of gravestones are here.

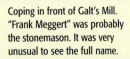

Coping in front of Galt's Mill. "Frank Meggert" was probably the stonemason. It was very unusual to see the full name.

Scotsmen were still working, and twelve of them had become contractors. Most of the Germans were also on the job, although some had absconded without reimbursing the company.

All earth moving was done by pick and shovel, using either horse-drawn dump carts or wheelbarrows. Stone was supplied by quarrymen using blasters, called "shooters," working with black powder. Much of the cutting and dressing of the stone was done in the winter, when masonry work and other construction was delayed or suspended. Carpenters were used extensively for the heavy timbers needed in the locks and lock gates—no easy task, since the matching gates (the width and height of a lock, with huge cantilever beams and heavy metal wicket gates near the bottom) were immense structures—and also for constructing the lock-houses, small work boats, bridges, and wooden dams.

Reconstruction of the old canal near Richmond got underway in 1838. This was more difficult and undesirable work than new construction. Cabell included in his annual report for that year a monthly list of the workers on this eastern canal. June had the greatest number with a total of 820, including 671 men and thirty-nine boys. Of this total, 462 were engaged in blasting rock.

In November 1836, for the new construction west of Maiden's Adventure, Cabell reported hiring 1,356 men and 361 horses. He added that pay for good laborers was $1 per day, paid monthly. A bonus of 20 percent was added for those orderly and industrious workers who persevered to the end.

Two years later Cabell noted that about two-thirds of the 800 laborers then employed were white men—the greater part of them foreigners recently arrived from various European workshops. Many were Irish immigrants who drifted to various public works in progress and "were constantly arriving and departing upon the different lines as interest and caprice dictated a change."

This "incongruous mass," as Cabell termed them, struck for higher wages in May 1838, and again in June. During the summer, the president complained, "the work was greatly retarded by the extreme heat and the inaptitude of the still pre-pondering [sic] mass of foreign labourers to withstand its debilitating effects." The Scots and the Irish especially suffered from the heat and humidity, unknown in their home countries, and they could not become acclimated.

Efforts to acquire more black labor were augmented by special agents, but they had little success. Moreover, nearly 100 members of the black workforce left when harvest time came. Cabell stated that in July of 1838, the heat "exceeded anything in the memory of the oldest men." On one day, some fifteen or twenty Irishmen expired in the heat and another 100 to 200 left for the North. The rest were prevailed upon to stay by the furnishing of a moderate portion of ardent spirits, the provision of small hospitals, and the attendance of a physician.

Not only laborers died: General John Hartwell Cocke of Bremo Plantation, a director, noted in his diary that he wanted a stone placed at the "feet of the graves of Brown and Wilson" who were buried on his estate, Bremo Recess. He directed that the stone be inscribed "Two Engineers, Brown and Wilson. The first was drowned and the 2nd died of Fever during their services in erecting the adjacent section of the Js. R. K. Canal—1836." The men were buried in the family cemetery, but there is no marker.

By the last quarter of 1838 Cabell reported the force was "more manageable and stable," consisting of about two-thirds blacks and one-third whites.

Colonel Bolling was never favorably impressed with the Irish. His diary for December 3, 1837, noted, "Took the stage at Hague's with a crowd of rough, filthy, stinking Irish stone masons, etc., amounting to 10 passengers inside and 3 out." He did not let this affect his sense of justice, however. For April 24, 1839, he reported: "Two Irishmen from the canal brought before me [on] a warrant for Dog Stealing whom I dismissed for no evidence."

At this time the Chesapeake and Ohio Canal was likewise having trouble with its Irish laborers, reporting them as quarrelsome, interrupting work to brawl, and driving off the skilled American mechanics and masons.

Finally slave labor came to be used extensively for both construction and maintenance work on the James. At one point, the company agreed to buy its own slaves to reduce the annual turnover of trained men, but this proved financially unfeasible. Normally slaves handled the relatively unskilled work, but because of the difficulties in obtaining good help, many were eventually trained for more skilled work.

In 1850 chief Second Division engineer Walter Gwynn noted in a report:

> In the southern country, where mechanics are scarce, the contractor is often compelled to pay exorbitant wages for those of inferior grade, and of bad character and habits, men who war against our institutions, and refuse to work with our slaves.
>
> The contractors on the canal estimate the superiority of slave labour over white labour, in cost of wages, as one to two, and in physical endurance and efficiency, in ratio three to two. Experience of the canal has proven that there is no portion of the work which cannot be executed by slaves. A few months teaching only is necessary to make them proficient in almost every part of the work.

Indeed, the stone for several of the locks had been prepared almost exclusively by slave labor—including the Judith Dam above Lynchburg, one of the most important structures on the line. In that case, the slaves were hired as common hands by the contractor, and in two or three months they were taught to quarry, drill, and cut stone quite as well as the majority of the white journeymen.

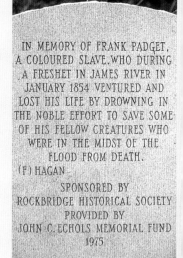

Replacement gravestone (above) for Frank Padget, a slave who drowned in 1854 in the Blue Ridge Gorge while attempting to save others from a flood. The original monument (below), now accessible in Frank Padget Memorial Park in Glasgow, was carved by James Fagan & Brother, Sculptors, in Lexington.

1840

Richmond to Lynchburg by Water

As sections of the canal were completed prior to the grand opening, small boats were using parts of it at no charge—more than 1,000 batteaux and riverboats, according to one report from Joseph Cabell. By November of 1840, water had been let into the whole line, and the canal to Lynchburg was nearly complete.

Considering it necessary and proper to make a personal inspection of the work, the "Directory" boarded, in Cabell's words, "one of the light and beautiful iron packets" at Richmond on November 11, 1840. This "iron packet" was named, appropriately, the *Joseph C. Cabell*. The party reached Lynchburg on the seventeenth, having had to transfer boats at the combined locks 46–47 below Lynchburg, which were not quite completed. A rope ferry at the locks pulled the boats across the river, as the canal changed sides. The Directory was satisfied, and the public was notified that on December 1 the navigation of the whole of the First Grand Division would be thrown open.

On December 3 the Lynchburg-owned freight boat *General Harrison* was the first craft to reach Lynchburg from Richmond. Little is recorded of canal traffic in the following months, although Colonel Bolling's diary notes that navigation was closed by ice from December 20 to January 8—not a very auspicious beginning.

The 146½ miles of this First Division, from Richmond to Lynchburg, took nearly five years to complete. The total cost was more than $5 million. Incidentally, it was not until this year [1840] that Nelson Tinsley finally started operation of the new cement plant at the Blue Ridge Dam.

Canal scene in Richmond

The Troubled Years

By 1841 work had progressed on the line above Lynchburg to the point that it was necessary to start rebuilding the old Blue Ridge Canal, built fifteen years earlier through the steep drop at Balcony Falls, in the Blue Ridge Mountains. Unfortunately this meant that the old locks had to be taken out of use in order to enlarge and reconstruct them—resulting in not only the loss of tolls, but also the loss of many boats with their cargoes, and sometimes even the loss of lives, in the rapids.

To make matters worse, on June 21 a storm of extraordinary violence caused considerable damage to the canal. This and a serious breach of the line in October delayed navigation on the First Division for more than three weeks. Yet revenues for this first year were still over $121,000, double those from river traffic the year before. Cabell anticipated doubling this figure again in 1842, but it was not to be.

By March 1842 the financial situation of the canal company had become so critical that the General Assembly passed an act granting a loan, contingent upon the company's stopping all new construction and cutting salaries. This prompted a meeting of the stockholders in May, during which the salary of the president was reduced to $2,500 and that of the chief engineer to $2,000.

1841

1842

The early Blue Ridge Canal through the mountains, plied by batteaux, would have looked like this before it was rebuilt and enlarged in 1841 to become a part of the JR&K. This drawing is an artist's conception of a similar early canal around the falls in Richmond. Batteaux like this—with a rudder instead of a steering oar—may have been invented by the artist.

1843

Disaster struck again on July 13, 1842, in the form of the greatest James River flood since 1795. Cabell said "the quantity of water discharged from the heavens in the space of ten hours is among the most remarkable that has occurred since the first settlement of the state." The damage this torrent left behind interrupted navigation for almost two months, cost $42,000 in repairs, and reduced tolls received for the year to under $100,000.

This may have been the final blow for Judge Wright, who had been on the job continuously since his return in May of 1839. A few weeks after the flood, the judge pronounced his health seriously impaired by the southern climate and returned to his home in New York City. It was supposed to have been a leave of absence lasting until the end of September, but Wright died in New York on August 24 at the age of seventy-two. His entire career proved so distinguished and influential that more than a century later, in 1968, the American Society of Civil Engineers noted his pioneering work and recognized him as "The Father of American Engineering."

William Lake, the able English engineer, had also become too ill to work and later resigned and returned to England. Thus, Edward H. Gill was made acting chief engineer in Wright's absence.

Besides savaging the canal itself, the 1842 flood also brought a fresh wave of criticism, particularly from the many railroad supporters in the Assembly and in the press. The president, the directors and the engineers—all were brought under fire again. A special committee of the General Assembly was appointed to study the whole record of the James River & Kanawha Company, and its report of over 200 pages was given in March 1843. It traced the history of the operation, construction costs, quality of engineering, and salaries, and also made comparisons with other canals. In the end, though, the conclusion was that all the company affairs had been properly conducted and the officers and engineers had served well and with dedication.

Even so, 1843 was not to be a good year. All new construction was cancelled; the job of chief engineer was eliminated, along with all the engineering staff—except for those placed in other positions. Edward Gill wound up accepting a position as one of two superintendents of maintenance, while still having responsibility for engineering work. His salary was $1,500 per year.

On April 14 another flood as high as the one the year before washed out the Hollins Mill Dam on Blackwater Creek at Lynchburg and damaged the canal aqueduct that crossed the creek below it. Before repairs had been completed, yet another flood occurred on September 17.

Typically hopeful, Cabell concluded that things couldn't get any worse. The September flood, he said, was the last of ". . . three great freshets which have occurred . . . within the term of fourteen months; a combination of events without parallel since the period of the revolution, and judging by past history of the stream probably to continue unparalleled for ages to come."

Edward Hall Gill was born in Wexford, Ireland, in 1806. In 1819, his immigrant father, Valentine Gill, became a surveyor on the Erie canal. Edward worked on four canal projects prior to coming to Virginia in 1838. Originally hired as principal assistant engineer under Charles Ellet, he served as chief engineer in 1842 and worked in that capacity until the position was temporarily eliminated in 1843. His relationship with the company continued on and off until 1852, when he became a superintendent with the Virginia Central Railroad. He died in Richmond in 1868.

Floods or "freshets" were a constant problem for the canal. This flood in 1936 overtook the lock house at the Lynchburg dam, still used at the time to control the city's waterworks canal. Note Scott's Mill in the left background (see page 16).

This year did see one exciting event—the introduction of a steam-powered packet boat, the *Governor McDowell*, which made a number of runs on the James River and Kanawha Canal. Alas, unusual damage to the canal banks was blamed on the action of its propellers. The next year a supposedly improved model with paddle wheels, the *Mount Vernon*, made one run on the First Division before authorities decided that steamboats were too detrimental to the canal. A few years earlier, the Chesapeake and Ohio Canal had lined some sections with stone to allow the operation of steam vessels, but the James River and Kanawha Canal was never financially able to do this.

The next year, 1844, was free of floods, but the elements still were not cooperating. Instead, the weather produced the greatest drought since 1806. The wooden dams leaked water so badly that navigation was affected all summer long.

Revenue on the First Division of the canal for this year totaled nearly $178,000. Expenses, maintenance and repairs came to over $54,000, leaving a net income of more than $123,000. Cabell was still optimistic, convinced that completion of the canal would bring similar income from all divisions, plus much more from all the through trade on a completed connection with the West that would encourage industry along the line.

Another investigative committee of the legislature reported they, too, could find no mismanagement. However, the company's plea for funds to resume construction was turned down by the General Assembly, who added insult to injury by ordering further reductions in salaries. The salary of the president was reduced to $1,500 for the coming year, with the proviso that if funds for construction were forthcoming this would be increased.

1844

1845

Cabell Resigns but Refuses to Quit

At a company meeting on February 3, 1845, Joseph C. Cabell was again unanimously elected president of the James River & Kanawha Company for the coming year. But at another meeting on March 7, the stockholders were told that Mr. Cabell had resigned his office of president on February 19. This resignation was accepted by the directors with "feelings of the liveliest regret," the group noting further "that his entire devotion to the best interests of the company, and the faithful and untiring discharge of his official duties, have in innumerable instances, placed him in positions adverse to sectional and personal interests, and thus given rise to prejudices against him, which are alleged to have the effect of preventing the legislation requisite to enable the company to proceed with its improvement."

Cabell's move was not a complete surprise, despite the seeming endorsement of February 3. At the December 1844 annual meeting, the president had received considerable criticsm for his operation of the company, and there was talk then that he might resign.

In his eleven years as president, Cabell had consistently pressed for a continuous waterway to the Ohio. His last annual report had continued to make this argument, listing eighteen engineering surveys made since 1810 and insisting "perhaps no other line of improvement whatsoever has been the subject of so great an amount of preliminary examination."

But this time the stockholders were not swayed, voting that the connection between the James River and the Ohio River should be by a continuous railroad. They further moved that the legislature again be petitioned for money to complete the work.

Cabell then appended to his annual report one of the most thorough and detailed reports possible to imagine. Entitled "Defence of the Canal and of a Continuous Water Line through Virginia," it totaled 272 pages and was printed in pamphlet form. It included observations from lengthy personal tours by himself and others to many northern railroads and canals over two summers. It compared costs of construction, operating expenses and income of the two forms of transportation. He quoted figures from the numerous surveys for both the canal and railroad. He had letters from iron furnace operators comparing the quality of their product with northern iron and cost advantages with a canal. Letters from geologists outlined other minerals and natural resources suitable for development that could best be hauled by water, at lower rates.

Cabell's interest and concern did not cease with his resignation and the publication of his extensive document. In 1851, when action appeared imminent on the railroad question, he prepared a forty-eight-page report outlining additional arguments in favor of the canal over a railroad.

Until his death in 1856 at the age of seventy-eight, Joseph C. Cabell remained convinced that a water route to the Ohio River would again make Virginia a great power among the states. It may well be that he was the greatest engineer on the line. Over many years, he had engineered the formation of the company, convinced the General Assembly to increase the initial financing, and continued to persuade them to finance and promote the work in the face of severe opposition and criticism.

Gwynn and Chittenden Rescue the Project

In 1846, with Cabell out of the picture, the stockholders proceeded to elect Walter Gwynn president of the company. Richard H. Toler, editor of the *Lynchburg Virginian*, was in Richmond to report on proceedings of the legislature (and to act as proxy for the Corporation of Lynchburg's shares in the canal company). On January 20, 1845, he had printed a letter from the Richmond newspaper opposing the re-election of Cabell and mentioning Major Walter Gwynn, then president of the Portsmouth and Roanoke Railroad, as Cabell's possible successor. According to the letter writer, Gwynn had "a high reputation as a civil engineer, and as a man of energy and talent."

The January 23 edition of the Lynchburg newspaper had a further note from Mr. Toler, who wrote, "at present Major Walter Gwynn the President of the Portsmouth Rail Road, is chiefly spoken of, though I am not aware that he has assented to this use of his name. He is a gentleman of fine talents, I understand, of great energy of character and of high attainments as an engineer—but whether, in other respects, he would be preferable to Mr. Cabell, I am not able to say."

Gwynn certainly appeared to be a good man for the job. He was born in 1802 in Jefferson County, now West Virginia. He graduated from West Point in 1822 and served ten years in the Army Engineering Corps. In 1832 he obtained employment with the Portsmouth and Roanoke Rail Road Company, which was beginning construction of its line from Portsmouth, Virginia to Weldon, North Carolina. By 1835 he was chief engineer, later became president, and served until the line was forced to close in 1845.

In the meantime he and three other engineers contracted in October 1845 to complete construction of the Chesapeake and Ohio Canal to Cumberland, Maryland in two years. Financial and labor problems stalled their efforts until 1847. The contract was canceled, Gwynn and one other partner withdrew, and work resumed under other arrangements.

While the salary offered in Virginia of $1,500 was not attractive, the position offered security and potential, and Gwynn entered vigorously into proving that canal transportation was superior to the railroads for this route. One of his first acts was to determine what was needed to proceed with the delayed construction above Lynchburg. During the summer of 1846 he made a personal inspection of the entire works to the Ohio River.

At the annual meeting in November 1846, Gwynn pressed for continuation of the water line to the Ohio in accordance with Cabell's plan. His estimate totaled nearly $11 million even though more than $5 million had been spent from Richmond to Lynchburg. He urged further that the state should finance this. The

1846

Major Walter Gwynn, the former president of the Portsmouth and Roanoke Railroad, became president of the James River and Kanawha Company in 1846. The following year he also accepted the job of chief engineer. Criticized by some legislators for assuming both roles and drawing two salaries, he willingly prompted the board to elect a new president in 1847. During his tenure Gwynn completed the work to Buchanan, through the most rugged section of the river. Though he championed the plan to complete the canal through to Ohio, Gwynn eventually left the company to become the chief engineer of the Blue Ridge Rail Road in South Carolina.

1847

W. B. Chittenden served as president of the company from May 1847 until his death in February 1849. He revealed in a deathbed confession that he had embezzled $11,000 from the company—money which his estate eventually repaid.

stockholders agreed to increase his salary to $2,500 for the coming year and to pay the travel expenses of his tour. He was then unanimously re-elected president.

In its March session, the General Assembly approved a loan to continue work on the canal. At the stockholders' meeting on March 17, Gwynn was made chief engineer of the company while still remaining as president. This carried an additional salary of $2,500, giving him a total compensation of $5,000. Although the Lynchburg newspaper reported "there was obvious economy in this arrangement—the professional attainments of Major Gwynn being of the highest order,..." some of the legislators were critical of his two positions and salaries.

President Gwynn promptly called a stockholders meeting for May to resolve the question, saying he was under no obligation to remain as president. At this meeting, W. B. Chittenden, who had served capably as secretary of the company since its formation, was elected president, and Gwynn was named chief engineer. C. O. Gerberding, assistant secretary, succeeded Chittenden as secretary.

In his first annual report in November, President Chittenden spoke of the rough times and appalling difficulties the company had faced, and said of Cabell's efforts: "No one . . . can truly appreciate the worth of the man whose undaunted and untiring energy in the conduct of the business of the company entitled him to the appellation of 'The Pilot Who Weathered the Storm,' although in doing so, as a last resort, he sacrificed himself with Roman devotion to its fury."

When Gwynn was appointed chief engineer, he rushed plans for getting the work under contract so as to complete the line as far west as the North River by 1849. The engineering corps was hurriedly reorganized and survey parties put in the field. One of the assistant engineers appointed was Edward Lorraine, who later succeeded Gwynn as chief engineer. By the first of October all the work was under contract.

Construction between Lynchburg and the North River, considered the most difficult on the line, was in the most trouble. All contracts for dams had been abandoned, along with many of those for locks and other work. Lack of capital, high labor costs, stone that was harder than expected, and low-bidding, inexperienced contractors had all contributed to the difficulty. Many contracts were re-let several times, and the chief engineer and his assistants were kept busy solving the problems and supervising the work.

Charles Ellet's original plans for this section called for wooden locks and dams, in accordance with his plan to save initial costs and get the line in operation more quickly. Major Gwynn, with the knowledge of the excessive burden of maintenance of such structures on the First Division, had decided the extra cost of cut-stone locks and dams was preferable. He planned for the two wooden dams on the old Blue Ridge Canal to be replaced and five new dams to be built, all of stone. As it turned out, finances and contract problems dictated that the two old dams would be retained as wooden structures, and one of the new dams also would be wooden.

Just prior to the annual meeting in November, word was received of an approaching financial crisis in Europe. This so disturbed the board that the work above the North River was temporarily postponed. Then, on November 26, another freshet, even greater than that of 1842, stopped navigation for a few weeks. Major Gwynn made a hurried inspection and estimated that repairs would cost $13,000.

Realizing the importance of a good supply of hydraulic cement for all the new construction, Gwynn tapped into his contacts with the Chesapeake and Ohio Canal and persuaded one of its men, Alexander B. McFarlan, to come to Virginia as principal superintendent of masonry. He then directed McFarlan to find a better supply of the blue limestone close to the cement plant at the Blue Ridge Dam. This meant, among other things, the termination of Nelson Tinsley's contract to run that facility.

Tinsley's replacement was Charles Locher, who had operated a cement plant in Cumberland, Maryland, on behalf of the C&O Canal. (Locher's family eventually purchased the Blue Ridge plant and ran it as the James River Cement Company until 1907.)

Oddly enough, given his background as a railroad man, Gwynn came to subscribe to Cabell's belief in a continuous water line over the mountains. His twenty-five years of experience in railroad engineering, he told the board, only enhanced his credibility in this regard.

President Mason Continues the Mission

President W. B. Chittenden, who had been in poor health for some time, passed away on February 12, 1849. On his death bed, he confided to two of the directors that he had appropriated company funds totalling over $11,000 to his own use. Secretary Gerberding had knowledge of this and had left by train for the North. He was never apprehended. Chittenden's estate eventually repaid his obligation, and this appears to be the only scandal among the many dedicated agents of the company.

On February 12 the board named one of the directors, Thomas M. Bondurant, to serve as acting president until the next stockholders' meeting. Then on May 9, John Y. Mason was elected president.

The new president came with impressive credentials, national political contacts, and the clout needed to carry weight with the General Assembly. A successful attorney, Mason had served in Congress as a representative from Virginia from 1831 to 1837. Following that service, he was appointed a circuit judge, then a Federal District Judge in Virginia. In 1844 President Tyler named him Secretary of the Navy, then retained him as Attorney General. Mason was again picked as Secretary of the Navy in 1846 and served in this capacity during the Mexican War. He had retired from the cabinet in 1849 to practice law in Richmond when he was elected president of the canal company.

Like Cabell and Gwynn, Mason was also a strong believer in the all-water route to the Ohio, and successfully persuaded the Assembly to continue financing its construction. In September he and the chief engineer made a tour of the

1848

1849

John Y. Mason, president from 1849–1853, had served in Congress, as a Federal District Judge, as Secretary of the Navy (twice), and as Attorney General before taking this post.
IMAGE COURTESY LIBRARY OF VIRGINIA

whole line. In 1849 the General Assembly approved three projects: to complete the Tidewater Connection in Richmond, to finish the canal connection between the Rivanna Navigation and the James River Canal, and to build bridges below Lynchburg to provide access to the canal from the south side of the river. All these directives cast another great load on the chief engineer and his staff.

Along with all the other work, surveys were done on the summit route over the mountains, primarily to determine the availability of an adequate water supply at the high elevation. Rain gauges were used and dams and drainage basins were calculated. The surveyors concluded that the water supply was adequate to pass 268 boats per day, far more than was anticipated.

Gwynn, who had been ridiculed for his use of rain gauges and for the whole summit plan, commented in his report that year: "But, on my part, truth is the great result at which I wish to arrive and I care but little in what position that places me in regard to the opinions of others, especially of those who with too much pride to study, and too much wit to think, undervalue what they do not understand and condemn what they do not comprehend."

President Mason, making his first annual report, urged that plans be adopted to proceed with the canal from Buchanan to Covington without delay. Meanwhile, work on the Second Division was probably at its peak. In May of that year workers were listed as: 663 white men, thirty-two free blacks and 1,325 slaves, for a total of 2,020.

That momentum was soon lost, however, when the half-completed Judith Dam was partially washed out during a moderate flood. This brought increased harassment from critics whose litany of complaints claimed that work was progressing too slowly, that it was costing too much, that it was not being properly supervised, that the engineers were not qualified, and that the chief engineer was not spending enough time on the job.

Judith was the first dam above Lynchburg, which is now known as Reusens Dam. (Much of the original lower stonework and part of the guard lock are still visible.) It had been nearly completed from the south side of the river, leaving a gap of about sixty feet near the north end. The high water rushing through this sluice washed out the stones like dominoes, each one loosening another, leaving a breach about 200 feet long.

Gwynn maintained there was no fault in the design, for which he took full responsibility. A special investigating committee brought in seven outside engineers or consultants, who agreed that this was an unfortunate accident. The committee, composed of noted engineers from other states, included "Professor Mahan of West Point, Professor Ewell of The College of William and Mary, Colonels Abert and Turnbull of the United States Topographical Engineers, Mr. Roberts of Ohio and Messrs. Jarvis and McAlpine."

The Second Grand Division Completed

Late in 1851 the Second Division was opened for traffic to Buchanan. While several years tardy in completion, it was generally well constructed through the most rugged section of the river.

1851

Meanwhile, the First Division, after eleven years of operation, had seasoned and had been repaired and maintained to the point that chief engineer Gwynn reported with pleasure, "the success which has attended the working of this important portion of the canal during the past year. It is without parallel in the history of canals in this country, and furnishes unmistakable evidence of the fact that time, which crumbled work of greater solidity and pretension, lends its hand to consolidate and mature the works of a canal for endurance and resistance of its ravages."

Yet the engineers could not rest on their laurels, for contracts had already been let for the first work on the Third Grand Division to Covington. Also, additional survey work was continuing on the critical Fourth Division over the summit level of the mountains.

Considering how much of the work involved on-the-job training, engineering errors were minimal. The most obvious one along the James concerned the lock joining the canal with the river at Cartersville, downstream in Cumberland County. After completion, it was found to be about ten feet too short for the larger boats to pass. While this received a lot of attention from the critics, it was only a matter of a few weeks—and no great extra cost—to dig out the pit and add to the stonework.

Edward Beyer lithograph of the canal just above the Blue Ridge Dam before entering the gorge, now at the town of Glasgow.
COURTESY TED TREVEY

One of the combined locks of the Tidewater Connection in Richmond was found to be about three feet short. This was corrected by notching the thick wall between the two locks by this length to take the bow of the few boats long enough to require it. And Judith Dam had to be raised one foot higher than planned because the sill of the lock above had been laid out a foot too high, and the error was not caught until too late.

When the canal was in operation, regular maintenance crews were required, directed by superintendents of maintenance who reported to the chief engineer. The ranks of these crews included slave laborers, stone masons, carpenters, cooks, boatmen, and others.

One of the chief problems was leaks in the canal banks, many caused by muskrats and crayfish. To prevent this, teams of slaves were assigned to patrol various sections and make regular checks. They were given a bonus if they detected trouble and prevented leaks from occurring, and also were allowed to sell the skins of any muskrats they could catch. As financial problems mounted and criticism of labor costs rose, though, these crews were reduced and supervision tightened.

Inside view of North (Maury) River Bridge showing the horse passageway and slot for the tow rope on the right.

View of the North (Maury) River Bridge, combined towpath and carriage way for Blue Ridge Turnpike. Note slot for tow rope in side of bridge.

Ezra Walker, the long-time agent on the James River and Kanawha Turnpike over the mountains, met this criticism in an 1843 report on how his crews operated: "A faithful man with from six to ten hands, with three or four yoke of draft cattle [oxen], a plough, scraper and other tools," was given a section thirty to fifty miles long. "All hires have been made by the month, twenty-six days of labour to constitute a month." It was "the peremptory duty of the manager, to see that the cook prepared breakfast for the hands by the dawn of day, so as to be eaten at Candlelight, prepare and carry out dinner at midday, and set their supper at candlelight in the evening, by which means the hands were not called from their labour from daylight till dark. By this regulation, about fourteen hours labor has usually been performed for a day's work. . . . The use of ardent spirits has at all times, been peremptorily forbidden. . . ."

He further pointed out that draft cattle were purchased each spring and sold in the fall, usually for what they cost, so the only expense was their subsistence. Under this type of management, the James River and Kanawha Turnpike consistently showed a profit from its tolls.

More Troubled Years

Year after year, the board and engineers presented their ideas about the feasibility of a canal route over the Appalachian Mountains to the Ohio. The idea never died. At the 1851 annual meeting, President Mason, and Major Gwynn in particular, presented strong arguments for a continuous water line rather than a railroad.

Included was a letter from Henry D. Bird, an engineer and president of the successful Petersburg and Roanoke Railroad. In regard to the cheapness of railroad routes, Bird said, "The ingenious gentlemen who sit at their desks and figure out how cheap railroads can carry, in my opinion do a great deal of mischief to the cause they advocate. In regard to their theory, they are like the worthy Frenchman, who had a favorite [theory] about some subject, and upon being told that it was not sustained by facts, replied 'so much de worse for de fax.'"

1852

The villain in the winter of 1850–51 was ice, which closed the canal the last half of December and the last half of January for a total of thirty-two days. The only consolation was that the rival Chesapeake and Ohio Canal had been closed for four months and the Erie for five months. Several large freshets did considerable damage and suspended navigation for several weeks on the First Division, while construction of the Third Division was exhausting funds, and stockholders were again calling for a reduction in personnel and salaries.

A special committee studied the difficulties and noted that the staff and salaries had already been reduced significantly. Nevertheless, it was recommended that the president's salary be reduced from $3,000 to $2,500, and the chief engineer's from $3,500 to $2,000.

In a counter report, however, the chairman of the committee objected to the top-level salary cuts, saying about the president, "I dissent; because it is not the physical and manual labor that is employed in this office, but the mental exertion, the political and moral influence which should be in the person of the president of the great improvement, not only of Virginia, but of the union and the world."

In regard to the chief engineer, he argued in part: "First: It cannot be expected to command talent equal to this work for the sum of $2,000. . . . It is respectfully suggested that this company, with from eight to twelve millions of money expended shall not descend to dealing with officials upon a picayune principle."

The stockholders agreed, and these salaries were not cut. The rank and file investors did not, however, agree on the Mason/Gwynn plan for a continuous water route. This year the railroad forces prevailed again, and a resolution was passed to complete the canal to or near Covington, then build a railroad to the Ohio River, leaving the company at liberty to complete the water line when practicable.

1853

President Mason called a special stockholders meeting in April 1853, advising that the General Assembly had taken the mountain railroad matter into its own hands. On February 15, the legislature had passed an act authorizing the Board of Public Works to construct a railroad over the mountains from near Clifton Forge as an extension of the Virginia Central Railroad.

The only concession was that this Covington and Ohio Railroad had to be laid out so as to reserve a right of way for the canal at a future date.

It is ironic that in 1853 Charles Ellet, Jr., former chief engineer of the canal, was made chief engineer of the Virginia Central Railroad that was then building the tunnel through the Blue Ridge at Afton under the supervision of Claudius Crozet. This line was to extend to Covington, and the Covington and Ohio Railroad was to become a part of it upon completion. While Ellet was not the leader for the mountainous part of the canal work, this authorized railroad line would ultimately defeat the continuous water line for which he had made so many strong arguments.

On March 2, the Assembly passed another act for a loan to allow completion of the canal to intersect the new railroad and to complete the Tidewater Connection at Richmond. In August, contracts were let for all the remaining work to Craig's Creek, fifteen miles above Buchanan.

The last day of August, Walter Gwynn—by then a colonel—terminated his services as chief engineer. His final report of that date commented briefly on the conditions of the works. It concluded with appreciation that a right of way had been left by the railroad for the future canal, and said, "For the water line will be carried through, and nothing can prevent it but the occupancy of the only available route."

Gwynn left to take a position as chief engineer of the Blue Ridge Rail Road Company in South Carolina. The *Lynchburg Virginian* of October 10 noted that he had tendered his resignation to take a position at a salary of $5,000. In 1857, under his direction, his new company completed the first tunnel in this country that was over a mile long. He died in Baltimore in 1882, the oldest West Point graduate.

Thomas H. Ellis and Edward Lorraine

In his annual report to the stockholders on October 24, 1853, Judge Mason said that circumstances required that he not be considered for president for the coming year. Just the day before, he had been appointed envoy extraordinary and minister plenipotentiary to France, a post he held until his death in Paris in 1859.

Thomas H. Ellis, a director, was elected to replace Mason. Edward Lorraine, engineer of the Western Division and D. W. Walton, engineer of the Eastern Division, jointly assumed responsibility for the engineering.

Edward Lorraine was born in New Orleans in 1818, but grew up in Richmond and graduated from The College of William and Mary in 1837. That year he started as a rod man for the canal on the James River, one of the young Virginians Cabell had said were hoping to make civil engineering a career. He soon became an assistant engineer, but in 1842 he resigned because of a disagreement. He later returned and spent the balance of his distinguished career with the James River and Kanawha Company.

In 1854 the Tidewater Connection in Richmond was finished, with five stair-step locks allowing boats to pass from the Great Basin down to the tidal water of the James River by way of the "Richmond Dock" and the Great Ship Lock. Two of the five staircase locks are still intact in a park in downtown Richmond.

Also, 1854 saw the Southside Railroad completed into Lynchburg from Petersburg, the first real competition to canal traffic on the James River.

By 1855 the enlargement of the canal at Lynchburg was underway, designed to provide more water for industry and with a separate feeder canal for the city waterworks. Financial problems were still mounting, but President Ellis concluded his annual report to the stockholders with these brave words: "Twenty years have now elapsed since the organization of the James River and Kanawha Company. Within that time, two hundred miles of inland navigation, unsurpassed by any of

Hired under Gwynn, Edward Lorraine started as a rodman and was quickly promoted to assistant engineer, and then engineer of the Western Division. Lorraine was perhaps the most devoted and hopeful of all the company engineers. Though he presided over the twilight of the project, he never gave up the dream of completing the canal as originally planned, over the mountains to the Ohio River.
COURTESY LIBRARY OF VIRGINIA

1854

1855

Mason Tunnel, 192 ft. long, one mile above open culvert. Here was a long horseshoe bend in the river. A tunnel across the neck would save three miles of canal. The tunnel was completed but not used by the canal. The railroad enlarged the tunnel and still uses it today. Aqueducts on the east and west were used to cross the river to reach the tunnel. The piers are now used by the railroad for their bridges.

the same description in this country, have been constructed." (He had conveniently forgotten about the Erie Canal, completed in 1825, whose length was 363 miles.)

The chief engineer reported work well under way on the Third Division and urged that the canal be completed to Covington rather than Clifton Forge, extending the length about ten miles farther west. The idea of making the canal climb the western mountains would not die, and a special committee presented another long and detailed report on the advantages of continuing the water line westward.

In the winter, navigation was closed for two months by ice, "a thing never before known in its history," according to the superintendent of repairs. The funds for completing the work to Craig's Creek were not provided by the legislature, and, as a consequence, all contracts were canceled as of the end of the year.

Construction Ends on the James

1856

By 1856 ten locks and several culverts had been completed above Buchanan, much of the stonework done by slave labor. On this third section the 192-foot Mason Tunnel, named for the former president of the company, had been dug through a ridge to save nearly three miles of canal around a long loop in the river. The 1,900-foot Marshall Tunnel, named for Chief Justice John Marshall, was to cut across the next large loop upstream to save another two-and-one-half miles. Workers were well along with vertical shafts dug from both ends and in the center of the tunnel, but all this work came to a halt when the state refused further funding. (Much of this work stands today almost as it was when abandoned.)

Marshall Tunnel, east end, never completed. Looking east from the inside, 25 ft. wide x 20 ft. high, approximately.

The Virginia and Tennessee Railroad was completed from Lynchburg to Bristol same year. The extension proved a desirable adjunct to the canal as it brought in western trade, much of which would, in theory, transfer to the canal at Lynchburg. Already, though, the Southside Railroad—in conjunction with the Richmond and Danville Railroad—was charging unrealistically low rates to take considerable freight business away.

This, then, was the end of all new construction on the canal except for completion of the North River Line up to Lexington. The North River Navigation Company, a private firm, had begun work on the branch line in 1850 but was unable to complete financing. The James River and Kanawha Company took over the remaining work in 1858 and finished the project in 1862.

Aqueduct piers were built to cross the James River to the east entrance of the planned 1,900 ft. Marshall tunnel to save 2.5 miles of canal around the horseshoe bend and beyond.

The company never gave up hope of taking up the work again and completing it over the mountains. Lorraine presented a beautiful map in one of his reports that showed the entire canal as planned to the Ohio River, including all locks and dams with elevations of the line over the mountains.

However, from this point on, the engineers' work consisted mainly of maintenance, repairs, and improvements to the existing line. Floods and other problems continued to plague the company.

Lorraine's diaries have interesting observations on day-to-day life. On February 4, 1853 he noted, "Went to town! Pray for what? to buy a chamber pot." On May 1, 1862, "Commenced packing up office, papers, books, etc. preparatory to running from the Yankees." (At this time the Federals were mounting their first threat to Richmond.) Later that year, "Moved to 'Bleak House' close to Lynchburg."

The Canal in the Civil War

The Civil War affected the canal less than it did the railroads. Not a piece of rail or rolling stock was available to the southern railroads during the entire war. The heavy traffic caused a rapid decline in the condition of their equipment; sections of railroads were often broken up by Yankee raids; and the wooden bridges were burned.

The canal, requiring mostly wood and stone, was better able to cope with repairs, although labor shortages caused increasing problems. Record receipts of over $445,000 were recorded for 1864, but being in Confederate currency it was not representative of actual value.

During the war the Confederate government operated twenty-five to thirty boats on the canal and confiscated boats for pontoon bridges. The Yankees did some damage to the canal in Goochland in 1863, but it was not until 1865 that the enemy inflicted any serious damage. In March General Sheridan's forces of 6,000 to 8,000 men damaged thirty-four locks from Bent Creek to Cedar Point, just west of Richmond. They made five breaches in the embankments and destroyed or burned numerous bridges, some boats, workshops, and the like.

In the two weeks prior to April 3, twenty-five miles of the line above Cedar Point had been repaired. Richmond was evacuated ahead of the Yankee invasion that day, and all repairs were stopped. The canal office at Richmond was burned and many valuable records were lost. Repair work was resumed on May 17, and after much deliberation and negotiation with the Federal authorities, the canal was opened through to Lynchburg a month later.

At the war's end, the board pushed necessary repairs to the line, and by the end of 1866 the whole system was in relatively good condition. In the meantime steps were taken to regain lost trade and to meet the increased threat of railroad competition. The board made arrangements with steamship companies to the north for advantageous combined rates.

Edward Lorraine wrote in his typical verse about an upriver trip from Richmond in wartime:

> On Friday last, at five, I got afloat
> on *Jefferson Davis* the packet boat.
> Twas crowded with men and soldiers in long boots,
> officers, privates, conscripts and substitutes,
> and women by the score with straw hats,
> and the usual number of squalling brats.

View on the canal near Balcony Falls. Rebel troops going from Lynchburg to Buchanan, on their way to western Virginia
HARPER'S WEEKLY, SEPTEMBER 28, 1861

The Last Twenty Years

In spite of its problems, as late as 1859 the company was the most powerful in the state. Total income that year was nearly $309,000 and disbursements about $153,000. Its freight tonnage was more than three times that of the Richmond and Danville Railroad, the most important rail line in the state, and only its large debt and interest on loans kept it poor.

The year 1859 also brought a surprising new prospect for completing the water line west, raising hopes yet again. A French group made an offer to buy the company in order to gain access to the coal and iron resources in the mountains. However, the Civil War began before details could be worked out, and after the war these plans failed to materialize.

The canal company persisted in its efforts and by 1867 was appealing to Congress to make it a national project. In 1868 a prospectus entitled "Central Water Line from the Ohio River to the Virginia Capes," written by Lorraine, aroused considerable interest. Iowa, Kentucky, Ohio and Kansas, all concerned about high freight rates to the East, petitioned Congress to undertake construction of an enlarged canal over the mountains.

Congress finally responded in 1870 and authorized a survey under the direction of Major W. P. Craighill of the Corps of Engineers. In the meantime, Lorraine had prepared a new scheme for crossing the summit level with a tunnel nine miles long and 200 feet lower than the two-mile tunnel originally proposed. He pointed out that this was not as difficult a feat as it might seem. By sinking vertical shafts every mile it would be, in effect, nine tunnels, each a mile long. Numerous locks would be saved and a more adequate water supply assured.

The Army Corps of Engineers was much impressed with Lorraine's plan, and he spent 1870–71 assisting them in the survey. The report was favorably received, but as usual, another survey with more details was ordered. Completed in 1872, the resultant plan envisioned an enlarged canal seven feet deep, carrying boats up to 280 tons. Total cost would not exceed $60 million, and it could be completed in six years. Plans for the tunnel were made by Benjamin Latrobe (son of the famous architect) and are on file in the National Archives. While the company had great hopes for the plan, the financial panic of 1873 assured its defeat.

Edward Lorraine died of smallpox on December 30, 1872, at his home in Richmond, at age fifty-five. Newspaper obituaries noted that he was a most amiable and estimable gentleman, and no one occupied a higher position as a practical and scientific engineer. While not well known outside the state, he certainly must have been the most loyal and dedicated of all the James River Company engineers. In addition, it appears he was the only one of the chief engineers who did not supplement his meager income with much, if any, outside consulting work.

The president at the time, Charles S. Carrington, noted in his report to the stockholders the next year: "Lorraine's love of truth and his moral courage, sound judgment and acquirements, his capacity for accurate observation, and his daily opportunity for more than a quarter of a century for the investigation of the

While stacks of railroad ties wait to be installed, packet boats still ply the canal above Richmond near the mouth of Tuckahoe Creek ca. 1881.

Last boatman on the James River and Kanawha Canal
COURTESY C&O HISTORICAL SOCIETY

1877

subject of hydraulic engineering, fitted him for great eminence in this the most difficult branch of his profession. . . . This gifted man devoted his life to duty with little concern for his personal advancement, and lived and died a consistent Christian."

James M. Harris, who had served as an assistant engineer and superintendent on the line above Lynchburg for a number of years, was appointed chief engineer and superintendent on April 1, 1873, at a salary of $1,500. He was to be the last of the chief engineers on the canal.

A hundred-year flood in 1870 had almost destroyed the company financially, although Lorraine had managed to have it restored to working order before his death. In a letter of November 1871 to William R. Hutton, chief engineer of the Chesapeake and Ohio Canal, Lorraine noted that repairs from the ravages of the flood were nearly complete and would total about $370,000.

This letter illustrates the rather free interchange of information between the different canal works. Lorraine adds in his letter that he would send an annual report to Hutton as soon as it was printed, and hoped Hutton would return the compliment. Many of the engineers moved from one canal to another and also to the railroads and back, as did many of the contractors and skilled laborers. Finances were a problem with most lines, and layoffs frequently dictated such changes. In addition, management personnel and the engineers frequently made tours of inspection of other lines.

As destructive as the flood of 1870 had been, however, the flood of 1877 was worse. It was, in fact, too much. While navigation was restored, the financial situation of the canal company was now impossible. In 1880 the Richmond and

Richmond and Alleghany Railroad, 1882, looking downstream from Big Island and Coleman Falls Dam. Canal, lock #5 and lock house are shown.

Alleghany Railroad Company was formed to take over the canal and lay down its line from Clifton Forge to Richmond, with the rails to be laid mainly on the canal towpath. Work started from both ends and met at Lynchburg.

The canal was kept open between the two sections and on the two branch lines, the Rivanna and the North River, while construction of the railroad was under way, and the navigations were busy with boat traffic carrying supplies for the railroad plus the regular traffic.

In August of 1881, the first through train service began and traffic on the canal was shut down. The Lynchburg paper noted that as the rail lines neared the town, the canal boats were being herded into the boat basin like "wild horses into a trap."

The canal along the James River closed just forty years after it began. The discussions of canal construction versus a railroad line had come to an end, and one feels the noise and smoke of railroad engines had been breathing down the necks of the canal workers for the whole forty years. Canal engineers were succeeded by the railroad engineers.

It is interesting to speculate what might have been if the engineers had been given the finances needed as construction progressed. Part of the problem was of their own making—their estimates of costs were usually low. However, if funds had been made available as needed, there is no doubt that a practical waterway could have been built across the Allegheny Mountains in ten to fifteen years. There is no doubt, also, that prior to the Civil War, a very substantial and profitable trade would have been established.

It was the old story of too little too late. The engineers acquitted themselves well.

1881

Lynchburg dam, guard lock and lockhouse. The lockkeeper controlled the flow of water to feed the mills and plants on the Lynchburg level below.

Lynchburg and Its Canal Era

"Lynchburg and Its Canal Era" was published by Gibson as his contribution to Lynchburg's bicentennial celebration in 1986. Although his focus is almost entirely on the city and the canal's role in its history, he broadens his treatment to cover Lynchburg's antebellum railroads. He later developed his article into a lecture on Lynchburg's transportation history, which he gave to dozens of civic and educational groups in the region.

This illustration shows the lower of two canal basins in Lynchburg. Note Southside RR and its bridge over the James River at left, and gauge dock in center background for charging tolls.

Lynchburg and Its Canal Era

On December 3, 1840, a large crowd gathered at the newly completed lower canal basin near the river below Ninth Street in Lynchburg. Excitement mounted as a distant boat horn was heard from down river. Soon a large freight boat, the *General Harrison*, came into view, drawn by its straining horses. A great cheer went up as it pulled in ahead of the rival boat it had raced from Richmond, according to the Lynchburg newspaper. Owned by the Lynchburg firm of Dolan, Kinnier & Co., it was the first boat to complete the 146½-mile trip over the "First Grand Division" of the James River and Kanawha Canal. Charles L. Mosby, a prominent local attorney and good friend of Joseph C. Cabell, president of the canal company, made a welcoming address. Standing on top of a boat cabin as he talked, he lost his balance and the cold water of the canal cut his speech short.

The improvements in river navigation made by the earlier James River Company, formed in 1785, had been less than satisfactory. Even with hundreds of batteaux being poled up and down the river, it was a difficult, expensive, and uncertain journey. Now, it looked as if the plan proposed by George Washington in 1784—joining traffic on the James with that on the Ohio River by a connection across the mountains to the Kanawha River—might be realized.

In 1829 Lynchburg had completed its new, modern waterworks, one of the earlier ones in the country. As a part of this project, under the direction of Pennsylvania engineer Albert Stein, a dam had been built just above the city on

THE Annual meeting of the Lynchburg Saving's Bank, will be held at their office, over the Store of Messrs. Martin, Ward & Davis, on Saturday the 29th inst. at early candle Light, for the purpose of electing Officers and Directors for the ensuing year.
JEHU WILLIAMS.
Dec. 24 1830

COURTESY JONES MEMORIAL LIBRARY

the James River. It stretched from the south bank across to the lower end of Daniel's Island just below the Federal-style mansion called Point of Honor. (A Lynchburg landmark, this fine home of Judge William Daniel, Sr. had been built by Dr. George Cabell, a first cousin of the company's president, Joseph Cabell.) When the canal company was formed in 1835 the city agreed to sell the dam to the company. In return, the canal company would maintain it and furnish the city the water it required for its waterworks.

Ironically, in June 1846, a flood washed out the poorly constructed dam. The company had to replace it with a substantial, curved stone dam.

Resident Chiefs

Early in 1836 Charles Ellet, Jr., then just twenty-six years of age, became chief engineer. Ellet was living in Lynchburg in charge of the work from the city to the Tye River. On October 31, 1837, Ellet married Elvira Daniel, the daughter of Judge Daniel, Sr., at Point of Honor. The young couple continued to live in Lynchburg while Ellet travelled extensively over the whole works and made visits to other canals. It was Ellet who was largely responsible for the design and construction of the first completed section of the canal. He was also responsible for surveys of a western route for a railroad over the mountains and improvements to the Kanawha River.

In 1838 Ellet hired an engineer working in Ohio, Edward Hall Gill, to direct these western surveys. Gill, thirty-two years old and born in Ireland, had served as chief engineer on two smaller canals and worked on three others. In that year Ellet also planned and got construction started on the line above Lynchburg to the Blue Ridge Gorge. During this construction period, the board of directors occasionally held their monthly meetings in Lynchburg to approve bids and examine the work. While very capable, Ellet was not personable and the board terminated his services in 1839. He was later to become famous as a bridge designer. In 1842 Gill was made chief engineer in charge of the work above Lynchburg and made his home in the city. Later his brother Washington Gill served as an assistant engineer.

Touring the Works

The canal below Lynchburg followed the south bank of the river in Campbell County downstream of the Mount Athos plantation, about twelve miles. The dam at Lynchburg supplied water for the six locks of this section down to where boats crossed by a rope ferry to the north side of the river above Joshua Falls Dam. In 1838, with construction progressing nicely, work was halted just below the city by John Percival, owner of the land later occupied by the Mead Paper Mill [now Rock-Tenn Co.]. Unhappy with the price received under condemnation proceedings, he threatened "certain and immediate death to any agent of the company"

Horseford Creek flows under Piedmont Flour Mill and railroad tracks. Part of the original canal culvert shown here is still visible from the river in 2009.

working on his land. An act of the General Assembly was required to overcome this major obstacle. As work progressed, enthusiasm for the canal mounted. In 1838 one of the local banks included a drawing of a lock and batteau in its newspaper ad.

At Lynchburg, the waterworks dam supplied all the water for the level below. A guard lock in the dam was operated by a lockkeeper to regulate the flow of water and pass boats up into the pond above. The company sold water to power the flour and planing mills and other manufacturing concerns along the canal in the city. At Blackwater Creek, a half mile below the dam, an aqueduct more than 100 feet long—with five spans of a wooden trunk resting on stone piers—carried the canal over the creek. The trunk was thirty-four feet wide and more than seven feet deep, and part of its rotted timbers are visible under the railroad bridge on the north end. The stone piers, with beautiful half-round capstones on the lower ends, are still intact. Just below this point the canal passed under a beautiful large stone arch bridge which carried traffic on Water Street (now Ninth) down to the toll bridge over the James River leading north to Amherst County. This stone arch was built for the canal by J. S. King in 1839, according to its inscription, and is still intact and carrying traffic.

Below the bridge, the canal widened out into a lower basin with heavy stone walls on each side. Here, warehouses handled the freight for loading and unloading boats. At the lower end of the basin a gauge dock was used to weigh the boats. Calibrated gauge marks on the boats were matched to a mark in the dock. These readings translated into the displacement of the boats and thus calculated their cargo weight. The toll gatherer used these calculations to charge appropriate tolls. Just below this point, Horseford Creek was carried under a mill (see illustration above) and the canal by a stone culvert. Part of this work is still visible on the river side.

Lynchburg from the east, circa 1850. The canal flows along the left bank of the river and the Southside Railroad crosses at center.

Also at the basin, water power was furnished to Hurt's Mill, which later became the Piedmont Mills. The stonework for this water supply is still visible in the basement. Several wooden bridges below the mills carried traffic over the canal. At Fishing Creek, just below the present paper mill, a large stone culvert set at an angle to the canal carried the creek under the canal. The upper end of this arched opening is still visible. Less than a mile below the culvert, lock No. 51 terminated the Lynchburg level. This lock is now completely buried under the railroad tracks.

Successes and Setbacks

During 1841, freight traffic on the canal developed rapidly, in spite of another June flood that did considerable damage in and below Lynchburg. Tolls for the year were more than $121,000. Boyd and Edmonds Co. of Richmond and Lynchburg started a line of light packet boats to carry passengers and mail between the two cities. Two of these, the *Joseph C. Cabell* and the *John Marshall*, made three trips weekly each way. The overnight trip took about thirty-three hours at a speed of four miles per hour. Fares charged were $8.00 each way, including meals.

For a period, daily trips were made and fares varied. In 1848 fares were reduced to $3.50 with meals extra. Frequent ads appeared giving fares and schedules for the packet boats. While the packets received the most interest, freight boats produced the major revenue. At no time were there more than six packets in opera-

The Phoenix Foundry, run by Albert Gallatin Dabney, was situated on the canal and, judging from this lithograph, made great use of it for freight. (See Beyer lithograph on page 85 for another view of the foundry.)

COURTESY ELIZABETH DABNEY HUTTER

tion, while 150–200 freight boats were operating. The larger boats were fourteen feet wide, more than ninety feet long and could handle up to eighty tons of cargo. This is an equivalent capacity to many of today's large railway freight cars.

The names of the freight boats were interesting and varied. They included the *John Randolph, Davy Crockett, Flying Lucy, Josephine, Lynchburg, Kanawha, Tennessee, Old Virginia, Old Dominion, Richmond, Ohio, Pocahontas, Buchanan, Red Bird, Lady of the Lake, Pig Iron*, and many others. Cargoes included grain, flour, pig iron, tobacco, lumber, whiskey, and farm produce. The trip to Richmond took about three days down and three-and-a-half days up for heavy freight boats. Average freight charges were $1.22 per ton for the whole distance or eight mills (8/10 cent) per ton mile.

In July 1842 a flood—according to President Cabell, the most remarkable since the settlement of the state—shut down traffic at Lynchburg for over two months. It did minor damage to the Blackwater Creek aqueduct. Then in April 1843 another flood almost as great struck, doing considerable damage but delaying traffic only a couple of weeks. On Blackwater Creek the Hollins Mill Dam and two wooden bridges below it washed out and lodged against the canal aqueduct but without causing serious damage. Again, a similar flood in September caused traffic to shut down for four days. President Cabell said three such floods in fourteen months was without parallel since the Revolution. Unfortunately, floods and lack of finances were to plague the company until its end.

The Ninth Street Bridge over the canal in Lynchburg was built by J.S. King in 1859. It provided a good vantage point for spectators at the re-enactment of Stonewall Jackson's funeral procession in May 2007. Most of the canal in the Lynchburg area has been filled in.

With new construction at a standstill after 1842, Edward Gill took a cut in pay and agreed to serve as superintendent of repairs for the upper half of the canal and provide such engineering as was needed. He continued to live in Lynchburg with his wife, Mary, a native of Pennsylvania. She especially was very active in St. Paul's Episcopal Church while he was most active in Masonic work.

In 1843 and again in 1844 Lynchburg was visited by two steam packet boats, the *Governor McDowell* and the *Mount Vernon*. The *Governor McDowell* was the first Virginia-built iron steamer and used an Ericsson-type screw propeller. Traveling at five miles per hour, these steamers not only created more waves but the action of their propellers created considerable turbulence, both causing excessive damage to the canal banks. The *Mount Vernon* was designed with twin paddle wheels to lessen the wake, but apparently the modifications were not effective enough. In addition, horse-drawn boats frequently engaged in illegal races with these steam-powered competitors, causing even more damage. The company decided it was not desirable to let them continue operating and transferred the steamers to the lower James.

Revenues were down in 1844 partly because of a very short tobacco crop at Lynchburg. A new lockhouse was completed at the waterworks dam in 1847. In late November, another great flood washed around the dam. However, damage on the whole was not great.

Later in the year Gill rejoined the engineering corps and was put in charge of the Tidewater Connection project at Richmond. His younger brother, Washington Gill, who had also come from canal work in Ohio, was working above Lynchburg and living at Bethel, just above Reusens. He married Mary Elizabeth Davies, daughter of Mayo Davies, whose home just off of present Trent's Ferry Road in Lynchburg still stands. Another younger engineer on this work was Edward Lorraine of Virginia.

Former canal at Lynchburg ca. 1935, now paved over.

N&W freight warehouse on right. Richmond & Alleghany freight house on left. Canal in center ca. 1935.

Headwall and locks of the dam at Lynchburg, ca. 1935.

Lynchburg Pump House feeder for waterworks dam.

Below: Lock gate from waterworks guard lock. This was used as a model for the restored Blue Ridge Parkway lock.

The fifty-mile stretch to Buchanan was completed in 1851. This added considerably to canal traffic. Built through beautiful but rugged country, it was a major engineering feat. Eleven dams were used in this short distance. Some of their more interesting names were Bald Eagle, Quarry Falls, Cushaw, Indian Rock, and Wasp Rock. That same year Lynchburg, requiring more water for its industry, was pushing the canal company to raise the height of its dams.

A major problem occurred with the Judith (now Reusens) Dam just below Judith Creek above Lynchburg. Before the heavy stonework was completed a small flood in December 1850 washed out much of the stone in the breach. This incident provoked severe condemnation by the canal critics. To resolve the blame, a number of noted canal engineers from all over the country assembled in Lynchburg and viewed the dam. Their opinion was

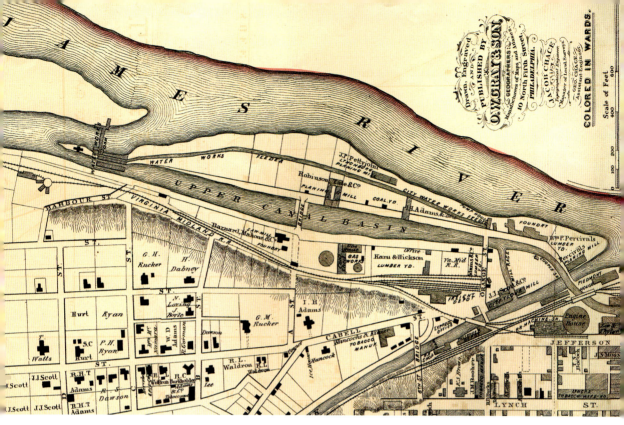

A detail of Gray's Map of Lynchburg, 1877, shows the upper canal basin, railroads and industries.

that it was an unfortunate set of circumstances and not faulty engineering. In fact, this stonework continues to serve as the base for the present power company dam.

Prior to its current use, the Judith Dam furnished water power for a steel rolling mill and a blast furnace at Virginia Nail and Iron Works and later for the iron smelting furnaces at Reusens. Just below this furnace site are the partial remains of lock No. 2. After the canal ceased operation, the local power company mounted a generator on this lock to supply the first electricity for Lynchburg. The remains are interesting because the first five feet were built earlier of wood-lined construction. The top, when completed, was made of solid stone. The two different types of construction are still readily visible. Much of this construction, including the beautiful stone masonry work, was done with hired slave labor.

The Rise of Rails

Even in the beginning, many of the canal stockholders, including those in Lynchburg, felt a railroad route was more practical than the canal. In 1846 the Southside Railroad from Petersburg to Lynchburg was organized. In 1848 the Lynchburg and Tennessee Railroad (later the Virginia and Tennessee) was formed to connect Lynchburg with the New River and Bristol. In 1854 the Southside Railroad was completed and took considerable passenger trade and some of the freight traffic from the canal. The trip to Richmond, including the transfer at Petersburg, took only nine hours by train compared to thirty-three by packet. That same year Edward Gill, having left the canal service, returned to Lynchburg as superintendent of the Virginia and Tennessee Railroad. Under the supervision of Gill the railroad was completed to Bristol in 1856. In contrast to the Southside Railroad this brought business in from the west and was an aid to the canal. In

Blackwater Creek aqueduct supplied water to Lynchburg mills after the canal closed. The flour mill on the right was fed by a millrace from the canal (see map on previous page).
PHOTO BY VAN NESS

Aqueduct's last days. C&O RY on right ca. 1935.

Aqueduct piers remain today and carry the main sewer line.

1860 the Orange and Alexandria Railroad reached Lynchburg from the north. The two years 1853 and 1854 showed total canal revenues exceeding $200,000 annually. Railroad competition and other circumstances prevented them from ever reaching this sum again.

The rapid growth of Lynchburg required additional docking area. In 1854 Judge Daniel, Jr. gave enough land below the waterworks dam to provide for an upper basin. That year six packet boats, 141 freight boats, and fifty-four batteaux were operating on the canal. In 1855 additional land was given by Judge Daniel to provide a feeder from the dam to the waterworks separate from the canal. Stephen C. Hurt, owner of Hurt's Mill, was contractor and the completion date of these major projects was 1857.

Superintendent James M. Harris, reporting on this, said Lynchburg "has the capital, an industrious and enterprising population. She has her railroads emanating from her, as a centre, almost in every direction. She has her canal to bring to her doors the heavy products of the mines and forests, and it does seem to me she is better situated than any other town in the state, if she could command the water power, to become a large manufacturing town."

In June of 1856, in just two weeks time, the regular maintenance crews of Harris replaced the complete wooden trunk of solid heart pine timber in the Blackwater Creek aqueduct. Harris said this structure was of no ordinary magnitude, being 143 feet long, thirty-four feet wide and eight feet deep. His carpenters and blacksmith did outside work when not busy on company jobs, bringing in

Blackwater Creek aqueduct from below, Virginia and Tennessee RR roundhouse and locomotive at left.

ALFRED BROWN PETTICOLAS SKETCH, 1858, COURTESY VIRGINIA HISTORICAL SOCIETY.

extra income for the company. Ice closed the canal for two months early in 1856, which was unprecedented.

In 1857 another flood did considerable damage at Lynchburg, including the new waterworks feeder. The need for more water power at Lynchburg required the company to start raising the Lynchburg level two feet higher. The waterworks dam and the dams connecting the islands above were also to be raised two feet. Again the canal and river froze over for nearly two months with ice twelve to fifteen inches thick.

In 1860 the company contracted to complete a dam from Daniel's Island across to the Amherst shore at Lynchburg. This would provide a greater and more permanent water supply for the city.

The start of the Civil War in 1861 had little impact on the canal except that a good many boats were taken off for use elsewhere. It also put off work on the dam. Several floods that year, however, required more than the usual repairs. The canal fared better than the railroads during the war. They were unable to get any steel for rails or rolling stock. As a consequence railroad operations were almost at a standstill by war's end.

The canal, except for Sheridan's raid in 1865 above Richmond (which did considerable damage that was quickly repaired), continued to operate in good fashion. In 1862 when the Yankees were marching on Richmond, Edward Lorraine brought his family to Lynchburg to escape the fighting. He had purchased a farm and brick house above Lynchburg he called "Bleak House." This, too, was on present Trent's Ferry Road, only a half mile from the Mayo-Davies home. It has since been torn down.

For Lynchburg the saddest occasion was the death of Confederate General Stonewall Jackson in 1863. His body was brought to the city by railroad and transferred to the packet boat *Marshall* for the trip to Lexington. A great crowd turned out to pay homage to this fallen hero.

Bleak House, farm home of Edward Lorraine near Lynchburg. Lorraine lived here during the Civil War while in charge of the Upper Division of the canal. Sketch by Lorraine.

Porridge Creek aqueduct at Stapleton in Amherst County below Lynchburg.
Culverts were full width of canal for smaller streams. Larger streams had aqueducts only twenty-one feet wide. Most were of stone but some had wooden spans.

ALFRED BROWN PETTICOLAS SKETCH, 1858, COURTESY VIRGINIA HISTORICAL SOCIETY

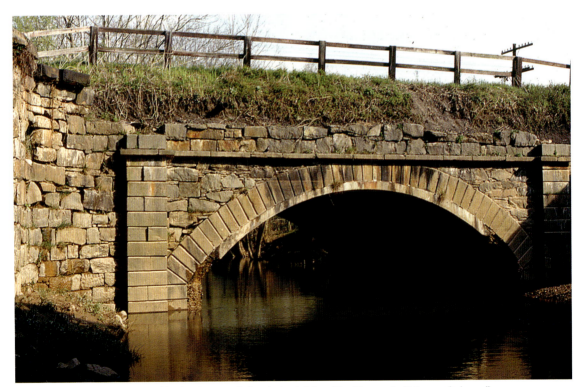

Porridge Creek aqueduct at present. Thirty-four-foot span. Railroad extended river side with concrete. Note curved wing walls.

The packet boat *Marshall* was a fine, large boat that had replaced the earlier *John Marshall*. Her captain in later years was James A. Wilkinson of Lynchburg. His son, James P. Wilkinson, served as mate under his father for some time. He became lockkeeper of the guard lock at the waterworks dam about 1875 and held this position until 1893 or later. Descendants of the family still live in Lynchburg. The *Marshall* ended her service on the bank of the James about a mile above the dam. She was used as a home for an elderly brother and sister until the flood of 1913 washed away the wooden superstructure. Her relic metal hull is now displayed in Riverside Park.

After the war, the canal company struggled financially to put the line back in good shape. In September 1870, the greatest flood of the century raged over nearly the whole line. Damages totalled about $370,000 and it took more than a year to restore all navigation. In 1872 the steel rolling mill at Reusens just above Lynchburg reopened, promising additional business. The Lynchburg and Danville Railroad was under construction, and the canal officers had allowed them to use part of the canal bed in the lower basin for their tracks. However, sharing the canal bed restricted boat passage and became a serious annoyance which took several months to correct.

Another great flood hit in November 1877, doing a great deal of damage at Lynchburg and above. While this was being repaired a smaller flood in September 1878 added to the problems. The company was financially insolvent and in despair. In 1878 the Richmond and Alleghany Railroad was formed to take over the canal company and replace it with a railroad from Clifton Forge to Richmond, including a branch to Lexington. Agreement was not reached, however, until 1880. Work then started on the new railroad.

Original curved waterworks dam at Lynchburg. Scott's Mill and its dam were added later. Note fish ladder between. These were required by the state to allow the shad to spawn upriver.

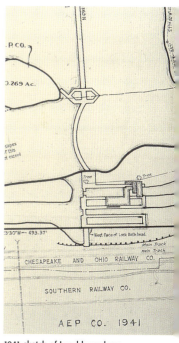

1941 sketch of Lynchburg dams and canal locks. Note fish ladder.

Lynchburg dam guard lock and lockhouse. Note Lynchburg waterworks feeder canal at right. C&O RY on left originally ran on towpath in most places.

In the meantime, repairs, which were at first thought impractical, were made to the canal. Under its agreement, the railroad was required to keep the canal in operation until they replaced it. At Lynchburg, they were also required to supply water for 100 years for businesses and the city on the Lynchburg level.

Canal traffic was stopped incrementally at both ends of the line as the railroad progressed. By late summer of 1881, the railroad was nearing Lynchburg from east and west. W. Asbury Christian, in his book *Lynchburg and Its People*, writes that "the dock at the foot of Bridge [Ninth] Street was crowded with freight boats, driven like wild horses into a trap."

On September 12, 1881, the 193-mile railroad was completed from Clifton Forge to Richmond. It was officially opened on October 15, as was the branch to Lexington. Below Lynchburg rails were laid using the old towpath as a roadbed for almost the entire distance. Above Lynchburg, variations were made in places to give more protection from floods. The Chesapeake and Ohio Railway, which took over the Richmond & Alleghany in 1891, gained the best grade to sea level of any railroad crossing the Alleghenies. The beautiful and substantial stone culverts and aqueducts, in most cases, continue to carry the tremendous pounding weight of daily freight trains, a real tribute to the skill and integrity of the engineers and stone masons of 140 years ago.

In 1883 the dam Lynchburg had wanted for so long was completed by the railroad across to the Amherst side. The waterworks dam that had been built in 1829 extended only to an island, providing enough water for the city's needs at that time. Lynchburg continued to draw water from the canal for its waterworks and industries until electric power finally supplanted water power. The C&O Railway continued to supply a lockkeeper to regulate water supply for the entire Lynchburg level and maintain the system. It was not until 1940 that they were able, through court action, to discontinue this service. Mr. Matthew Proffit served as their lockkeeper from 1899 until his death in 1936. His daughter, Mrs. Hester Butchard (later Fleshman), continued in his stead until 1940. At that time the lock house was torn down, water was drained from the level for the last time, and the canal bed in Lynchburg was filled in, just one century after it had been opened.

Virginia and Tennessee RR roundhouse and shop buildings. In the foreground is the covered bridge from Ninth Street to Amherst County.

ALFRED BROWN PETTICOLAS SKETCH, 1858, COURTESY VIRGINIA HISTORICAL SOCIETY.

Though the canal bed in Lynchburg was filled in, the rest of the canal was not, as can be seen today. The railroad agreed to keep water in the canal to furnish water to mills and other industries elsewhere along the river. This was done for many years.

Lasting Impact

Lynchburg was never to see the tremendous trade that would undoubtedly have come its way if the dream of Joseph C. Cabell for a great central water route could have been completed before the railroads became prominent. However, the forty years of canal operation was an important factor in the development of the city. Scottish, Irish, German, English and others as well as slaves worked on building and operating the canal. Some of these immigrants settled in Lynchburg, and many of its citizens can trace their ancestry back to those that had some part in this interesting era in the city's history.

The 1846 waterworks dam and the newer dam both remain intact and beautiful. Point of Honor, now preserved as a Virginia Historic Landmark and open to the public, still looks down on them from the hill above. The stone-lined water inlet feeder for the waterworks also remains intact and operational, but not open to the public on the upper end of the Griffin Products plant. The guard lock is buried under railroad tracks. Still visible and accessible are the Blackwater Creek aqueduct stonework, the stone bridge at Ninth Street, and parts of the culvert below. Judith Dam has been incorporated into Reusens Dam but its stone base and the upper and lower ends of the guard lock are still visible. Just below it, the double, eight-foot stone arched culverts carry Sugar Tree Creek under the railroad. Below this the interesting stonework of the upper end of lock No. 2 is still intact. Further down, Pigeon Creek empties into the river under a large fifteen-foot stone culvert visible from both sides. Just outside the city limits, to the east, the beautiful and large Opossum Creek culvert is readily accessible by the side of Rt. 460. The second largest culvert built, it spans twenty-four feet wide and is more than 100 feet long. Every stone is still intact. Perhaps someday these historic monuments will be developed into significant recreational areas.

Excursion packet boat on the James River and Kanawha Canal. The photograph was taken at Tuckahoe one week after the delivery of the first ties to the Richmond and Alleghany Railroad.

PHOTO COURTESY LIBRARY OF VIRGINIA

Canal Boats

69

"Canal Boats" makes use of miscellaneous data Gibson Hobbs collected over three decades of work on the canal. Romantic horse-drawn packet boats along the canal captured his interest as they do canal fans everywhere. The Canal Register, recovered from fragments of Lynchburg newspapers, sheds light on the variety of passenger and freight vessels that traveled the canal and docked in Lynchburg. The accompanying sections of an Edward Beyer drawing of the canal in Lynchburg were annotated by Gibson and the publisher. These are valuable resources for historians and Gibson wanted them included and available to everyone who shared his interest. The views of the re-created James River Batteaux on the river give perspective to the story of the canal and are representative of what Gibson hoped might be achieved with the canal itself.

Towpath bridge over Maury (North) River.
PHOTO BY A.H. PLECKER

Canal Boats

The *Lynchburg Virginian* newspapers on file at the Jones Memorial Library contain much canal-related material of interest. Unfortunately the issues for August 1840 through July 1841 are missing. Since the first canal boat arrived at Lynchburg from Richmond on December 3, 1840, according to the company records, the Lynchburg newspaper accounts of these first days are not available. The first issue of the paper on file after 1840 is dated August 2, 1841. A number of advertisements and other notes in this and later issues give information on the canal boats and their operations at Lynchburg. This paper was biweekly at the time.

Prior to the opening of the canal to Lynchburg, a great deal of freight was carried up and down the river on batteaux. These were wide, flat-bottomed boats propelled by poles. Until the canal was completed to Buchanan, all traffic above Lynchburg was still carried on them. Some batteaux continued to be used on the river between Lynchburg and Richmond and no doubt some made use of at least parts of the canal. Some of the batteaux were quite large and had captains and names just as did the canal boats. It is not clear from the newspaper listing of boats whether these included only canal boats or whether some batteaux were also included.

71

Packet Boat *Marshall*, Queen of the James River and Kanawha Fleet. This boat carried the body of General Stonewall Jackson to Lexington, VA, for burial in 1863. It was the last of the canal boats to enter Lynchburg and was beached on the south bank of the James River one mile above the city and remained there until it was carried away by the flood of 1913. The remains of the old hull (90' x 14'), constructed of galvanized iron, are on display at Riverside Park. The last owner and captain was James A. Wilkinson and the last mate was Captain Wilkinson's son, James P. Wilkinson.

Views of *Marshall* on a bank near Lynchburg. It was used as a home until the wooden superstructure was washed away in a flood.

President Joseph C. Cabell, in his 1854 report to the twentieth annual stockholders meeting, stated that the total number of boats operating on the canal was as follows: For transportation, seventy-five decked boats, sixty-six open boats, and fifty-four batteaux, totalling 195 boats and requiring 423 horses and 867 men. The average value of these boats with their teams was $1,000, $500 and $25 each respectively.

The numerous and economical batteaux were not horse-drawn but man-powered by crews who propelled the boats with long poles. In contrast, the six packet boats available for passengers, each with an average value of about $2,270, required 120 horses valued at $15,000 in addition to a crew of ninety-six men.

The canal boats consisted mainly of freight boats with lengths up to ninety to ninety-five feet, widths up to about fourteen feet, drafts of about four feet maximum, and capacities of eighty tons. The depth of the water in the canal was specified as a minimum of five feet. However, for the first several years after 1840, according to company records, it was not more than four feet deep in places. It is probable that many of the earlier boats were shorter and narrower, with less draft and capacity.

Only a few packet boats were required to handle all the passenger traffic. It is probable that the earlier ones were smaller in size and capacity than later ones.

Asbury Christian in his book *Lynchburg and Its People* states, "In February (1841) a line of packet boats was established between here and Richmond. Boyd, Edmunds & Co., agents, announced that on Monday, Wednesday and Friday of each week, at 7:30 A.M., the *Jos. C. Cabell*, Captain Huntley, and the *John Marshall*, Captain Hull, would leave alternately for Richmond, fare, eight dollars."

Boyd, Edmunds & Co. was a Richmond firm with an office in Lynchburg. The ad was continued in subsequent issues for the balance of the year, as are other ads mentioned below. In the report of president Joseph C. Cabell to the stockholders of the James River & Kanawha Co. at their sixth annual meeting in Richmond in December 1840, he mentions canal boats in the start-up of operations earlier in the year as follows:

> Soon after the general introduction of the water, boats began to move upon different parts of the line. On the 4th of October, one of the tight and beautiful iron packets belonging to Messrs. Boyd & Edmonds of Richmond, returned with passengers from the town of Columbia to the city of Richmond. [It is likely this was the *Joseph C. Cabell* and modesty caused him to omit the name.] On the 31st October, *The General Harrison*, a freight boat of large class, belonging to Messrs. Dolan, Kinnier & Co. of Lynchburg, and another boat of similar description, the property of the same company, arrived at Joshua Falls Dam below Lynchburg, and took on loads of flour, with which they descended the canal. On the 18th November, a freight boat belonging to Messrs. Shepperson & Co. of Scottsville, arrived in Richmond with a cargo of 300 barrels of flour from the town of Scottsville.
>
> On the 3d day of December, in consequence of the notification given, the freight boat *General Harrison*, accompanied by a similar boat, both laden with merchandise from the city of Richmond, entered the basin at Lynchburg, and were received with cheers and acclamations by the inhabitants of the town, who had assembled to witness their arrival.

A large packet boat in the basin at Lexington after Gen. David Hunter's attack in June, 1864. Notice the burned out barracks of Virginia Military Institute in the background.

In reference to the above, Asbury Christian's book states that a race from Richmond had been arranged between a Whig and a Democratic boat. The Whig boat, the *William H. Harrison*, won the race amid great cheers from the crowd.

A second ad in the August 2 newspaper about freight boats reads as follows:

NOTICE
The subscribers on the 1st day of March, 1841, formed a co-partnership under the firm and style of
BOYD, EDMOND & CO.,
for the purpose of carrying freight on the James River and Kanawha Canal, where we now have running SIX FREIGHT BOATS of the first class. We will also attend to the Receiving and Forwarding of MERCHANDISE and to the buying and selling of the same at the customary rates. Our Warehouse being situated on the banks of the Canal, will save to customers the additional expense of drayage. Our Mr. Boyd and Mr. Montgomerie will reside in Lynchburg. We beg leave to refer to the following gentlemen: (References in New York, Richmond, Lynchburg, Abingdon and Wytheville)
JAMES M. BOYD
ROBERT EDMOND
HUGH MONTGOMERIE
ISAAC DAVENPORT. JR.
B., E., M. & D.
April 8

A third ad, in the same paper, listed the names of two freight boats as follows:

A CARD
DOLAN, KINNIER & CO.,
Return their sincere thanks to their friends and the public generally, for the very liberal encouragement they have received since they started their line of
BOATS on the CANAL,
And beg leave to state that they have now established a Receiving and Forwarding House in Richmond, on the north side of the Basin, a little above the Toll House, under the same style and firm, to operate in connection with their line of boats and their House in Lynchburg and any Goods or Produce consigned to their care, will receive their strict attention, and will be forwarded with the utmost despatch. Any produce shipped by their line of Boats, consigned to other Houses, will be carried through, with equal expedition, to any other line of Boats on the Canal. They have just started two more splendid Boats, the DAVY CROCKETT and JOHN RANDOLPH, and, will, in a few weeks, have finished and under way, two more, making their line consist of six superior BOATS. Their facilities being thus complete, and intending to devote their whole attention to the business, they respectfuly solicit a share of the public patronage.
March 22

As an experiment, a modern batteau passes through the restored canal lock at the Blue Ridge Parkway.

Since 1986 the James River Batteau Festival has promoted an eight-day batteau run from Lynchburg to Maiden's Landing, now with stops in Galts Mill, Bent Creek, Wingina, Howardsville, Scottsville, Slate River, and Cartersville, a distance of about 120 river-miles.

In the first years of the festival, the boats started at Lynchburg's Williams Viaduct (right). This bridge replaced the original covered bridge and a later metal truss bridge. The viaduct was replaced by the John Lynch Bridge, a modern, high level bridge. Photo circa 1986.

Bill Trout (right) and fellow batteauman at Lynchburg during the first Batteau Festival

The bottom of the hull of a batteau as found in Richmond's Great Basin. This one was heavily built to carry coal from the mines just west of Richmond

Canal Register

The listings on the following pages are reproduced just as they appeared in the *Lynchburg Virginian*, including the misspellings, errors, and typographical mistakes.

It will be noted that while the packet boat *Jos. Cabell* is shown there is no listing of the *John Marshall* in these registers. Whether it was out of service because of lack of business, repairs, or it did not come up as far as Lynchburg is not known. The ad listing it in operation with the *Jos. C. Cabell* continued throughout the year.

Only in the Register of August 12, 1841, was the listing of tonnage and tolls of the freight boats included. It will be noted that captains were sometimes changed or rotated on some of the boats. In 1857 Mr. E. L. Chinn was superintendent of repairs of the First Division. This covered the line from Richmond to Joshua Falls Dam. His summary of work done during the year was in Colonel Thomas H. Ellis' president's report to the stockholders in October 1857. Mr. Chinn said his force was divided into thirteen squads of various types of workers, and that in addition to other duties his carpenters had "fitted up the interior of the supply boat *Joseph C. Cabell*." He said of his hands employed as boatmen "three work the supply boat." He also mentions a cook for the supply boat.

He further states that "being able to carry most of the company's freight and officers in its own boat, promises, I think, from the experiment thus far, very favorable results." This latter probably refers to the supply boat *Cabell*.

It seems likely that this supply boat was the original *Joseph C. Cabell* packet boat converted to this service. It is probable that it had been replaced with a more modern and expensive boat.

Lynchburg, Virginia, 1855
by Edward Beyer
COURTESY JONES MEMORIAL LIBRARY

An interesting listing of canal boats titled Canal Register first appears in the August 9, 1841, issue of the *Lynchburg Virginian* and is continued in most of the issues thereafter. These list the name of the boat followed by the name of the captain. These are as follows for 1841:

August 9, 1841

ARRIVED:
Columbia, Devinny; Ohio, Jameison; Jno. Randolph, Crumpecker; Jos. C. Cabell, Lockett.

CLEARED:
5th—Wm. L. Lancaster, Harrington; Flying Lucy, Staton.
6th—Josephine, Lilly; Jack Downing, Lewis; Columbia, Devinny.
7th—John Randolph, Crumpecker; Commerce, Branham; Lynchburg, Fields.

August 12, 1841

ARRIVED:
Aug. 9—Kanawha, Snedaker, with 16 tons paying $58.23 toll; Tennessee, Bailey, 17 tons, $49.34; Elizabeth, Wilson, 21 tons salt, $44.44.

CLEARED:
Aug. 10—Tennessee, Bailey, 42 tons $151.02; Kanawha, Snedaker, 41½ tons $137.95; Old Virginia, Taylor, 35 tons, $106.67.

August 16, 1841

ARRIVED:
Aug. 12th—Wm. L. Lancaster, Harrington; Old Dominion, Pamplin; Holker
Aug. 13th—Jas. Madison, Peters; Buchanan, Armsworthy.
Aug. 14th—Enterprise, McGiffin; Lynchburg, Fields; Richmond, Eubank.

CLEARED:
Aug. 11th—Victoria, Perkins; Pioneer; Pellet; Exchange, Graves.
Aug. 12th—Elizabeth, Wilson.
Aug. 13th—Raleigh, Cowell; Highlander, King; Clayton & Burton, Ash; Mountaineer, Staton; Wm. L. Lancaster, Harrington.
Aug. 14th—Columbia, Devinny.

August 19, 1841

ARRIVED:

Ohio, Jameison; Pocahontas, Grant; Josephine, Lilly; Union, Jenks; Champion, Puryear; J. C. Cabell, Lockett; Farmer, Crouch; Mohawk, Quarles; John Randolph, Crumpacker; Flying Lucy, Staton; Kanawha, Snedaker; Davy Crockett, Doughty; Jack Downing, Huckstep.

CLEARED:

Aug. 14th—Old Dominion, Pamphlin; Holker, Beale; Enterprize, McGriffin.

Aug. 16th—Jas. Madison, Peters; Richmond, Eubank.

Aug. 17th—John Randolph, Crumpecker; Farmer, Couch.

August 23, 1841

ARRIVED:

Pioneer, Pellet; Highlander, King; Virginia, Minor; Tennessee, Bailey; Elizabeth, Wilson.

CLEARED:

Aug. 18—Champion, Staton; Ohio, Jamieson; Lynchburg, Fields; J. C. Cabell, Doughty.

Aug. 19—Union, Jenks.

Aug. 20—Pocahontas, Grant; Virginia, Minor; Mohawk, Quarles; Davy Crockett, Phelps; Kanawha, Snedaker.

August 26, 1841—No Canal Register included.

August 30, 1841

ARRIVED:

Old Virginia, Taylor; Old Dominion, Childress; Gen. Harrison, Clarke; Wm. L. Lancaster, Harrington; John Randolph, Crumpecker.

CLEARED:

Aug. 26—Experiment, Goodwin.

Aug. 27—Elizabeth, Wilson; Gen. Harrison, Clarke.

September 2, 1841

ARRIVED:

Kanawha, Snedaker; Flying Lucy, Staton; Raleigh, Cowell; Claytor & Burton, Ash; Davy Crockett, Crumpecker; Mountaineer, Staton; Highlander, King; Holker, Beale; J. C. Cabell, Lockett; Buchanan, Armsworthy; Richmond, Eubank; Josephine, Oberson.

CLEARED:

Aug. 28—Buchanan, Armsworthy.

Aug. 30—Lynchburg, Fields; Ohio, Cloas.

Aug. 31—Kenawha, Snedaker; Flying Lucy, Staton.

Sept. 1—Richmond, Eubank.

Gauging Dock for canal boats

13th St.

Lower Canal Basin

James River

September 6, 1841

ARRIVED:
Champion, Staton; Mohawk, Quarles; Tennessee, Bailey.
CLEARED:
Sept. 1st.—Highlander, Lockett.
Sept. 2nd—Pocahontas, Grant; Claytor & Burton, Ash; Ben Franklin, Pamplin
Sept. 3rd—Davy Crockett, Phelps; Champion, Staton; Mohawk, Sneed; Holker, Noell.
Sept. 4—Josephine, Oberson

September 9, 1841

ARRIVED:
Buchanan, Armsworthy; Lynchburg, Fields; Ohio, Jemison; Gen. Harrison, Clark
CLEARED:
Sept. 6—Wm. L. Lancaster, Harrington.
Sept. 7—Enterprize, McCriffin; Old Dominion, Childress; Pioneer, Pellet
Sept. 8—Buchanan, Armsworthy.

September 13, 1841

ARRIVED:
Ohio, Cloar; Exchange, Bland; Jos. C. Cabell, Doughty; Gen. Harrison, Clark.
CLEARED:
Sept. 9th—Lynchburg, Fields.
Sept. 10th—Gen. Harrison, Spiller.
Sept. 11th—Ohio, Cloar.

No Canal Registers were included in the September 16, 20, 23, 27, 30 and October 4, 7 11, 14 and 18, 1841 issues. The President's Report to the Seventh Annual Meeting of the Stockholders in December 1841 mentioned that a break in the canal near what is now Six-Mile Bridge on October 1 suspended traffic for about three weeks. From the above dates it appears that some other cause may have suspended travel for nearly the same amount of time in September. In June a severe storm and flood had done considerable damage and suspended traffic for some time until repairs could be made. The papers made no mention of any canal problems.

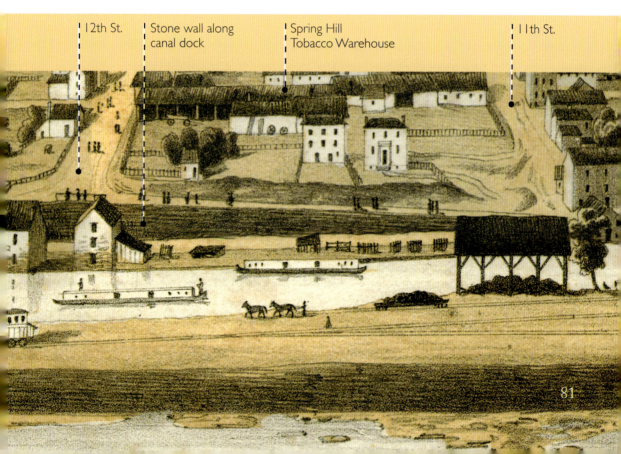

October 21, 1841

CLEARED:
Oct. 18—Kanawha, Jenks; Old Virginia, Taylor; Jack Downing, Murrill; Jno. Randolph, Crumpecker; Wm. L. Lancaster, Harrington.
Oct. 19—Abingdon, Dolan; Jos. C. Cabell, Doughty; Josephine, Orberson; Davy Crockett, Phelps; Highlander, Locket; Columbia, Harrington; Buchanan, Peters; Experiment, Goodwin; Flying Lucy, Staton.
Oct. 20—Lynchburg, Fields; Pioneer, Pellet; Claytor & Burton, Ash
Oct. 15—Lady of the Lake, O'Connor; Union, Jenks; James Madison, Peters; Farmer, Couch.
Oct. 16—Genl. Harrison, Clarke
Oct. 19—Tennessee, Baily; Wm. L. Lancaster, Harrington.

October 25, 1841

ARRIVED:
Oct. 22nd—Old Dominion, Childress.
CLEARED:
Oct. 21st—Experiment, Goodwin
Oct. 22nd—Old Virginia, Taylor; Buchanan, Armsworthy; Highlander, Locket; Josephine, Orbeson; Old Dominion, Childress.

October 28, 1841

ARRIVED:
Oct. 25th—Pocohontas, Grant; Red Bird, Brown
Oct. 26th.—Commerce, Brown
Oct. 27th.—Richmond, Eubank
CLEARED:
Oct. 25th—Columbia, Devinny.
Oct. 26th.— Clayton & Burton, Ash; Jno. Randolph, Crumpecker.
Oct. 27th.—Lynchburg, Fields

November 1, 1841

ARRIVED:
Oct.29th—James Madison, Peters; Gen'l. Harrison, Clark.
Oct. 30th—Tennessee, Baldly; Wm. L. Lancaster, Harrington.
CLEARED:
Oct.28th—Red Bird, Brown; Davy Crockett, Phelps.
Oct.30th—Richmond, Eubank.

November 4, 1841

ARRIVED:
Nov. 1st—Gabriel Tar, Pamplin; Buchanan, Armsworthy.
Nov. 3rd—Old Dominion, Childress; Jos. C. Cabell, Doughty; Lady of the Lake, O'Conner; Mohawk, Quarles.

CLEARED:
Oct. 30th—Jas. Madison, Peters.
Nov. 1st—Gabriel Tar, Pamplin
Nov. 2nd— Gen. Harrison, Clark; Wm. L. Lancaster, Harrington.
Nov. 3rd—Farmer, Couch; Tennessee, Baily.

November 8, 1841
ARRIVED:
Columbia, Devinny
CLEARED:
Nov. 4—J. C. Cabell, Doughty; Highlander, Fourqurean.
Nov. 6—Buchanan, Armsworthy; Mohawk, Quarles; Old Dominion, Childress.

November 11, 1841
ARRIVED:
Nov. 9th—Pocahontas, Grant
Nov. 10th—Jas. Madison, Peters; Richmond, Eubank.
CLEARED:
Nov. 8th—Elizabeth, Roberts; Lady of the Lake, O'Conor.
Nov. 9th—Experiment, Goodwin; Red Bird, Brown; Josephine, Orbeson; Lynchburg, Fields; Columbia, Devinney; Abington, Dolan.

November 15, 1841
ARRIVED:
Nov. 12th—David Crockett, Phelps; Pioneer, Pellet.
Nov. 13th—Gen'l Harrison, Clarke.
CLEARED:
Nov. 12th—Pocahontas, Grant; John Randolph, Crump
Nov. 13th - Richmond, Eubank; Jas. Madison, Peters.

November 15, 1841
ARRIVED:
Nov. 15—Claytor & Burton, Ash; Tennessee, Bailey.
Nov. 16—Wm. L. Lancaster, Harrington; Highlander, Fourqurean.
CLEARED:
Nov. 16—Pioneer, Pellet; Gen'l Harrison, Clarke; Old Virginia, Taylor.

November 22, 1841
ARRIVED:
Nov. 17—Jos. C. Cabell, Pryor.
Nov. 19—Red Bird, Brown; Lynchburg, Fields.
Nov. 20—Josephine, Orbeson.
CLEARED:
Nov. 18—Highlander, Locket; Tennessee, Bailey.
Nov. 19—Jos. C. Cabell, Dolan.

November 25, 1841

ARRIVED:
Nov. 20—Gabriel Tarr, Overton.
Nov. 22—Mohawk, Quarles.
Nov. 23—Richmond, Eubank; Columbia, Devinney
Nov. 24—John Randolph, Crumpecker; Abingdon, Pryor; Old Dominion, Childress.
CLEARED:
Nov. 20—Josephine, Orbeson
Nov. 22—Wm. L. Lancaster, Harrington.
Nov. 23—Lynchburg, Fields; Gabriel Tarr, Overton; Red Bird, Brown.

November 29, 1841

ARRIVED:
Nov. 24—Gen. Harrison, Clark
CLEARED:
Nov. 24—Columbia, Devigny; Pig Iron, Trent; Old Dominion, Childress.
Nov. 25—Buchanan, Armsworthy; Richmond, Eubank.
Nov. 26—Farmer, Couch; Clayton & Burton, Ash.

December 2, 1841

ARRIVED:
Nov. 29—Pioneer, Pellet.
Nov. 30—Elizabeth, Roberts.
Dec. 1—Jas Madison, Peters.
CLEARED:
Nov. 27—Mohawk, Quarles; Gen. Harrison, Clark.
Nov. 29—Abingdon, Dolan.
Dec. 1—Jas. Madison, Peters.

December 6, 1841

ARRIVED:
Dec. 4—Highlander, Lockett
CLEARED:
Dec. 3—Pioneer, Pellet.
Dec. 4—Kanawha, Snediker.

December 9, 1841

ARRIVED:
Dec. 6—Red Bird, Brown.
Dec. 7—Buchanan, Armsworthy; Lynchburg, Fields; Richmond, Eubank.
CLEARED:
Dec. 6—Experiment, Goodwin.
Dec. 7—Highlander, Lockett; Jas. Madison, Peters.
December 13, 1841—No Canal Register Included.

December 16, 1841
ARRIVED:
Dec. 13—Old Dominion, Childress; Pig Iron, Trent.
Dec. 14—Gen Harrison, Clark; Mohawk, Quarles; Jones, Nelson.
CLEARED:
Dec. 11—Buchanan, Armsworthy; Old Virginia, Taylor.

December 20, 1841
ARRIVED:
Dec. 15—Farmer, Capt. Crouch.
Dec. 17—Abingdon, Capt. Crumpecker.
Dec. 18—Pioneer, Capt. Pellet.
CLEARED:
Dec. 15—Pig Iron, Capt. Dixon.
Dec. 16—Columbia, Capt. Devinney; Gen'l Harrison, Capt. Clark; Gabriel Tar, Capt. Shaw.
Dec. 17—Mohawk, Capt. Quarles.

Ad from *Boyd's Directory of Richmond City*, 1867
COURTESY VIRGINIA CANALS AND NAVIGATIONS SOCIETY

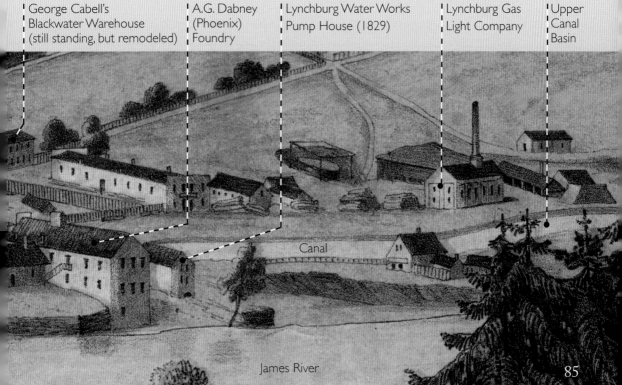

A canal and town, probably imaginary, from the canal company's five-dollar bill (see page 7)

Canaling on the Jeems and Kanawhy

Leighman Hawkins was a well-known Virginia newspaperman and historian. "Canaling On The Jeems and Kanawhy" has been abridged from an article Mr. Hawkins wrote for *Virginia And The Virginia County*, and was reprinted in the January 1951 issue of *Tracks*, a C&O magazine.

Richmond canal basin

Canaling on the Jeems and Kanawhy

by Leighman Hawkins

There was quite a bit of excitement at Richmond's canal basin. It was 7:30 p.m., and the packet *Harvey*, under Captain Charles, was due to leave for Lynchburg. Friday, June 25, it was, and passengers and the people seeing them off had been gathering since seven. They came in carriages and buggies. Some even came on foot.

Captain Charles was spoiling to get away. A full load of sixty passengers was about to delay his leaving and Lynchburg was a hundred forty-seven miles, fifty-two liftlocks, and thirty-three hours up the "dear old muddy Jeems."

As the sun dipped under a golden horizon, the last patron stepped aboard and Captain Charles gave the order to cast off. Strong-armed crewmen poled the boat from the dock, and those aboard and ashore began waving and shouting good-bye. There was laughter, of course, but some of the smiling eyes were moist. Very hospitable, these Virginians, and parting always was sad.

At the upper side of Seventh Street bridge, two horses were hitched to the towline. The driver boy, riding the rear horse, got the well-groomed steeds off at a smart clip. Fresh horses were stabled every twelve miles, each team trained to trot for all the dozen miles. Captain, steward, steersman, driver boy, cook, waiters and several deck hands make up the packet's crew.

The long, graceful boat rounded Penitentiary Hill at the average speed of about four and a half miles an hour. Most of the travelers stayed on deck to see Richmond fade in the distance.

First call for supper filled all seats in the saloon. It would take three calls to feed the passengers in crowded but nice quarters. The saloon (or main cabin) served as a living and dining room by day and as a sleeping compartment at night. There also were the captain's room, crew's bunkroom, cook's galley, toilet—and a small barroom where the finest whiskey—neat or mixed—was served. The white boat was eighty feet long and fifteen feet wide above the waterline. The fare from Richmond to Lynchburg was $7.50, including berth and meals. Children and servants traveled at half fare.

With supper over, men sought the cool breezes of the top deck to smoke (or chew) and talk. A few went to the bar for an after-supper brandy. Ladies, for the

Packet boat schedule printed in *The Richmond Whig*, Monday, November 4, 1872
COURTESY VIRGINIA CANALS AND NAVIGATIONS SOCIETY

Captain Dick Wooling's packet boat at Lynchburg, possibly leaving on a day excursion to Lexington

Serious Accident on the Canal.
GALLANT CONDUCT OF A PACKET CAPTAIN.

This morning as the packet-boat Madison was about twenty miles from Richmond, on its down trip, an elderly gentleman, who had been doing rather too much for one man towards liquidating the State debt by the Moffet-Punch law, fell overboard into the canal. The cries of the passengers aroused Captain Henry Wooling, whose duties had not allowed him to retire to rest until just a few hours before. The Captain sprang from his berth to the window of his cabin, and realizing at a glance the cause of the alarm, leaped fearlessly into the water, reached the toe-path in an instant, and running swiftly to the spot where the drowning man had sunk, dived after him, brought him to the surface, and held him safely there until the boat could be stopped and further assistance rendered.

This gallant feat was performed, it might be said, in the twinkling of an eye, so that the unlucky passenger was fortunately rescued without sustaining the slightest injury. In fact, he himself denied that his clothes were wet. Capt. Wooling, however, sustained a very painful injury in his right foot from which he will doubtless suffer for some time, though it is to be hoped that he will not be prevented from attending to his duty. It is evidently such acts of gallantry as this, together with his untiring courtesy, that have made Capt. Henry Wooling the most popular captain on the line, and his boat the people's choice.

REPRINTED FROM *THE TILLER*, COURTESY VIRGINIA CANALS AND NAVIGATIONS SOCIETY

most part, stayed in the cabin—reading, gaming or conversing.

As the last diner quit the saloon, the steward and his aides began making up the cabin for the night. Berths, in tiers of three along both sides of the walls, were let down and fastened with heavy straps. Berths were lowers, middles, and uppers, each a heavy frame interlaced with rope which held the mattresses. Dining tables were pushed together and fitted with bedding. That's where extra passengers slept when all the berths were taken. A heavy red curtain divided the saloon into two compartments—the front for women and children and the rear for men and boys. Upper berths were

Model of packet boat *Marshall* by Theodore Haxall of Richmond

avoided when possible. They were too close to the ceiling of the deck on which strode the captain and crew at all hours of the day and night.

Master George W. Bagby, thirteen, was aboard. Kids and servants got the upper berths and George was no exception. He, in later years, told how it was up there.

"As the shadows deepened, everybody went below. There was always a crowd in those days, but it was a crowd of our best people. I was little and it took little room to accommodate me. Everything seemed as cozy and comfortable as heart could wish. Being light as cork, I rose naturally to the top (berth), clambering thither by the leather straps with the agility of a monkey, and enjoying as best I might the trampling overhead whenever we approached a lock. I didn't mind this much, but when the fellow who snubbed the boat jumped down about four feet, right on my head, as it were, it was pretty severe. Still, I slept the sleep of youth. We all went to bed early. A few lingered, talking in low tones; the way passengers, in case there was a crowd, were dumped upon mattresses placed on the dining tables. The lamp shed a dim light over the sleepers, and all went well until someone—and always there was someone—began to snore."

The main cabin of a packet boat
FROM "A WINTER IN THE SOUTH,"
HARPER'S NEW MONTHLY MAGAZINE,
SEPTEMBER 1857

Throughout the night the trahn-ahn-ahn of the packet horn could be heard as lock after lock was approached. These blasts, made on a long tin horn, were signals for keepers to get their locks ready for lifting, or for lowering when the trip was downstream. The driver boy used a short one, something like those they sell at Christmas, to signal for a fresh team or to warn other craft of his presence. But the captain did his stuff on a giant of from six to ten feet long, which could be heard for miles across the countryside. Each captain had an individual twist to his horn blowing, and lock-keepers, even residents along the river, could tell which packet and which captain was coming up or down the canal.

Sunrise Saturday found the packet near Stokes, in Goochland County, forty-three miles out of Richmond. Green cultivated fields passed slowly in majestic review—mansion houses, barns, stables, smokehouses and slave quarters adding a backdrop to the ever-changing scenery.

Packet horn

"We turned out early in the morning," said George Bagby, "and had little room for dressing. The ceremony of ablution was performed in primitive fashion. There were the tin washpans and big tin dipper in the bucket of murky water. And there were the towels, a big one on a roller, with a pile of little ones—all of them wet."

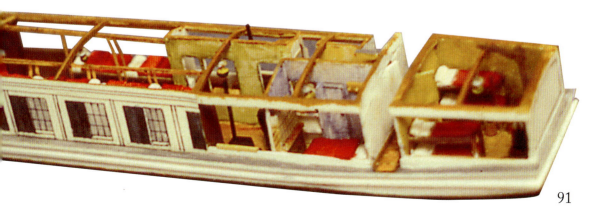

The packet boat *Marshall* on the canal near Lynchburg

The ladies' cabin during the day
FROM "A WINTER IN THE SOUTH,"
HARPER'S NEW MONTHLY MAGAZINE,
SEPTEMBER 1857

Passengers took turns washing face and hands and combing their hair. Then they lounged on deck until breakfast was called. the fresh morning air was mingled with the savory smell of coffee and bacon cooking on the charcoal stove in the galley. Those who looked into the cook's cramped quarters saw that there would also be oatmeal, wheat cakes, frog-eye gravy and golden-brown biscuits.

After breakfast scarcely a soul stayed in the ship. Almost all the passengers sought the crowded decks to bask in the sun. They now were seeing the James in all the splendor of its peace and beauty.

These shallow-draft boats had two decks—the decking on top of the compartments and the deck around the boat just above the waterline. Steps to the top deck were at the rear, between the last two compartments. Scenery could best be seen from there, and aside from the frequent cry of "Braidge! Low Braidge! Below everybody!" There was nothing to disturb those who sat there.

When there was a big bend in the river, the boat would let the passengers off so they could exercise their legs with a walk across country, catching the boat at the end of the turn or at the next lock. As the day wore on, a steady change was taking place in the scenery. They would soon be past the gentle lands of the low country. They were getting near the Blue Ridge foothills. The farther they went now, the more rugged the people.

The *Harvey* reached Scottsville at noon Saturday, eighty miles from Richmond, and a fresh crew took over. All, that is, except Captain Charles, who practically lived on his boat.

The only time the passengers paid much attention to the operation of the boat was when "locking through" or when passing another boat, which was often. When tow boats passed, the one coming downstream had the right of way. The

boat going up steered to the far (or berm) side of the canal and stopped so the towrope would fall slack into the water and flat on the towpath. The down boat and team could then pass over the up-boat's towline without stopping. A steersman had to be on duty night and day, his job being to maneuver properly when passing and at other times to keep the boat in midstream.

Supper Saturday night was called at about the same time as the night before. There was, however, a complete change of menu, and the bar did more business. Packets had one good advantage—they could pick up fresh provisions at almost any place along the river—ham, fresh eggs, milk, butter, green vegetables, poultry, all the things Virginians love.

A little before sunup Sunday, the *Harvey* rounded the deep curve below Lynchburg and passed up the canal toward the basin. On the right was a high cliff on whose brow stood tall pines and aged oaks. To the left were the hilly streets of the city. It was a bright, pretty morning—and early—but even at that hour a crowd was on hand to usher the boat in. The *Harvey* made the trip on time. The skipper said it was exactly 4:30 when the packet nudged over to the dock and was snubbed to the mooring post.

This trip of the *Harvey*, in 1841, was as far as the James had been canalized. Work even then was being rushed on improvements to Buchanan and to Lexington. This was Virginia's stupendous effort to capture a major share of the rich trade with the Midwest. It was an effort to make Virginia a shipping empire and put Richmond among the great ports of the world. To paraphrase George Bagby: "The canal was going to—well, it was going to do just about everything. And no respecting skipper or crewman ever called it anything but the "Jeems and Kanawhy."

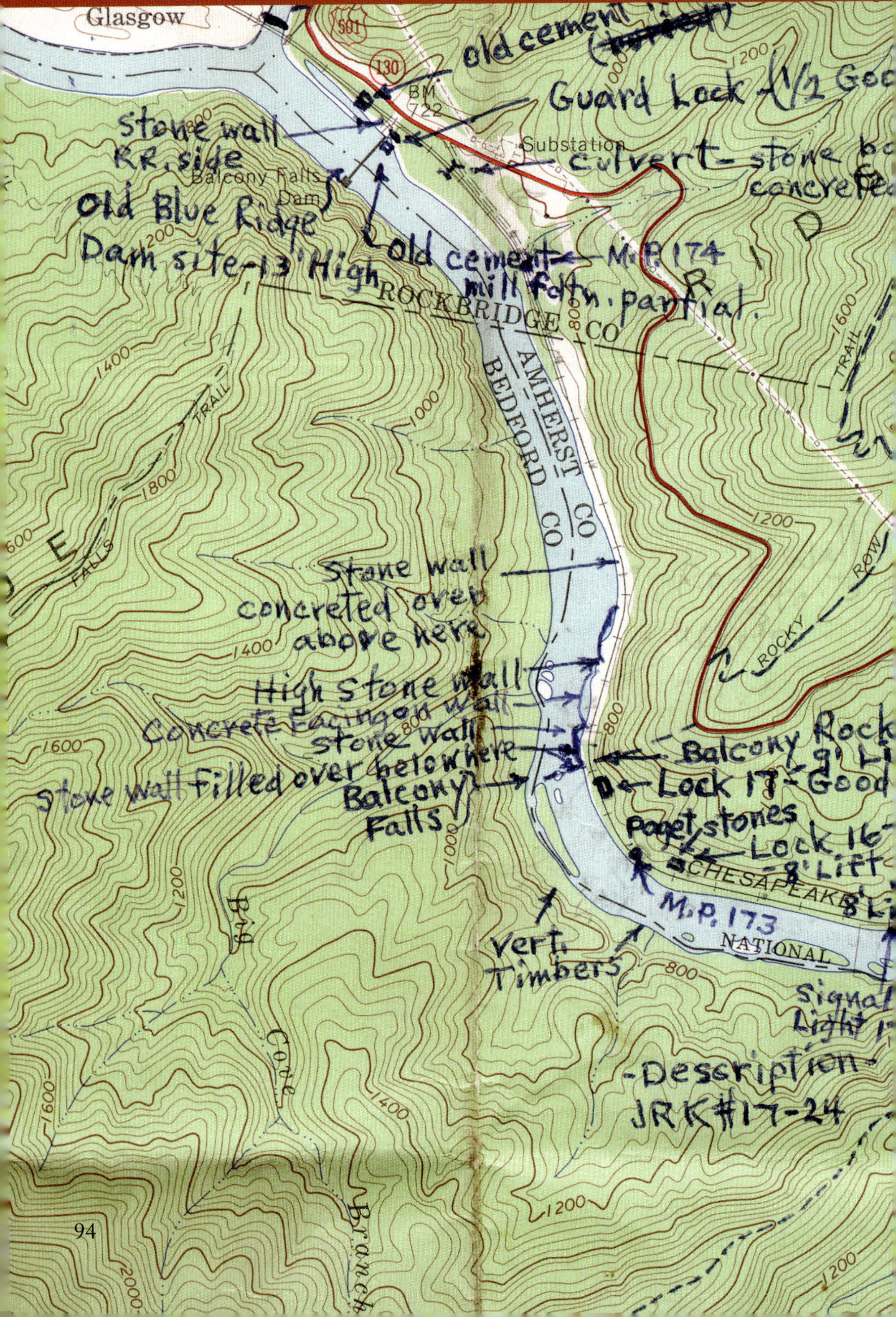
Glasgow
501
130
old cement
Guard Lock 1/2 Good
BM 722
Substation
Stone wall RR. side
culvert - stone box concreted
Balcony Falls Dam
Old Blue Ridge Dam site - 13' High
old cement mill fdtn. partial.
M.P. 174
ROCKBRIDGE CO
AMHERST CO
BEDFORD CO
1200
1400
1600
1800
1000
800
TRAIL
FALLS
Stone wall concreted over above here
High Stone wall
Concrete facing on wall
Stone wall
Stone wall Filled over below here
Balcony Falls
Balcony Rock
Lock 17 - Good
Paget stones
Lock 16
8' Lift
CHESAPEAKE
M.P. 173
NATIONAL
Vert. Timbers
ROCKY ROW
Big Cove Branch
Signal Light
-Description-
JRK#17-24

Maps

Maps

These maps consist of every documented feature along the James River and Kanawha Canal and are based on Gibson's notes and hand drawn sketches of the right of way. While the construction of the canal progressed from east to west, these maps are logically arranged from west to east, from Eagle Rock to Richmond.

Some of the thousands of photographs he took are included here as part of the record he left behind and the sites are indicated on modern USGS topographic maps to make this data more useful to readers. Additional information has been drawn from *The Upper James Atlas*, and *The James River Batteau Festival Trail* by William E. Trout III.

If you choose to explore some of these sites, please respect the rights of property owners. The railway line is dangerous, and trespassing on it is illegal. The river itself is beautiful, but it also can be treacherous. Enjoy the hunt, but please be careful.

Gibson's original maps are now housed at the Jones Memorial Library in Lynchburg.

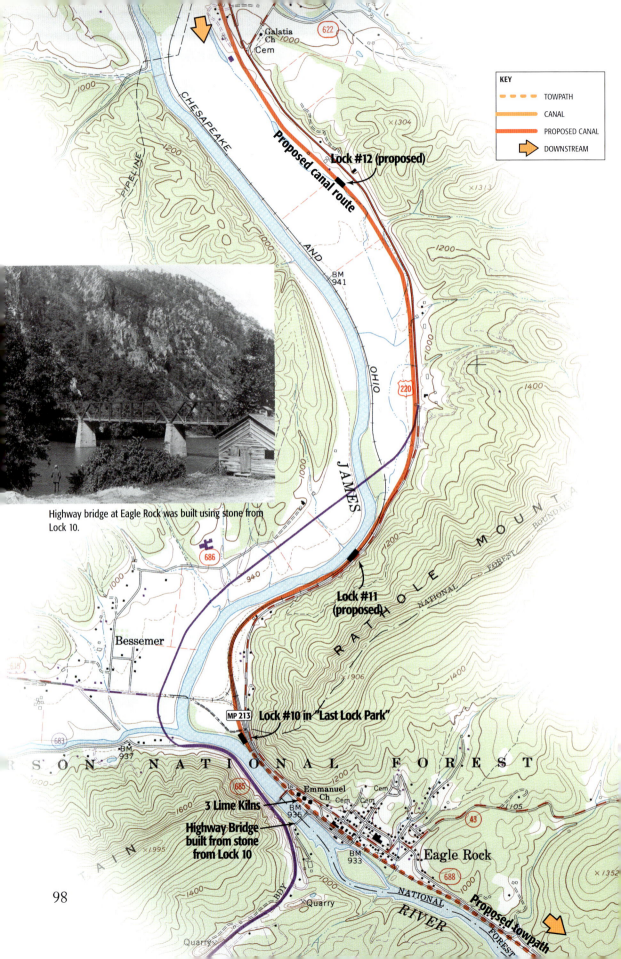

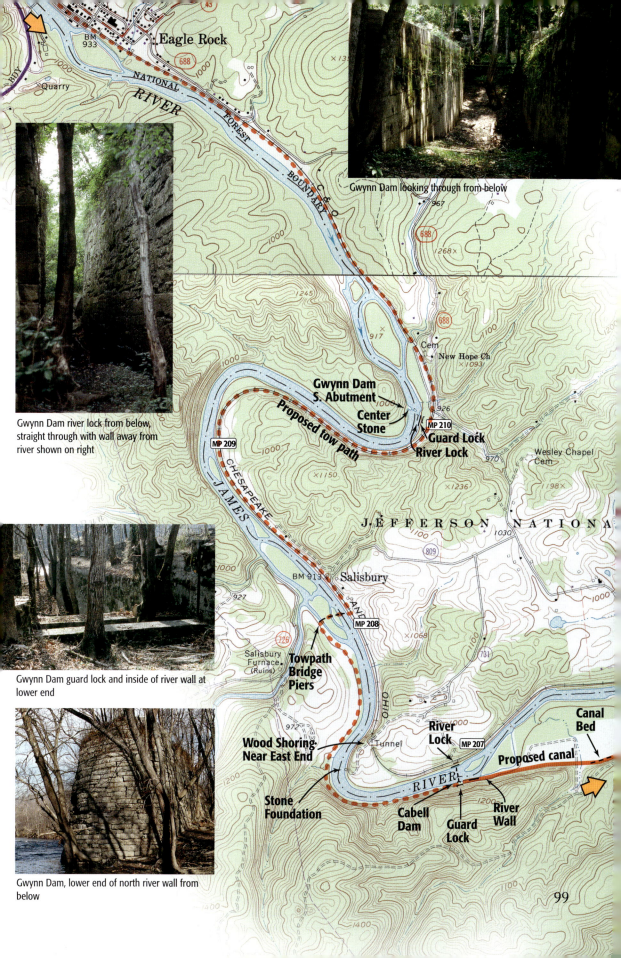

Gwynn Dam looking through from below

Gwynn Dam river lock from below, straight through with wall away from river shown on right

Gwynn Dam guard lock and inside of river wall at lower end

Gwynn Dam, lower end of north river wall from below

99

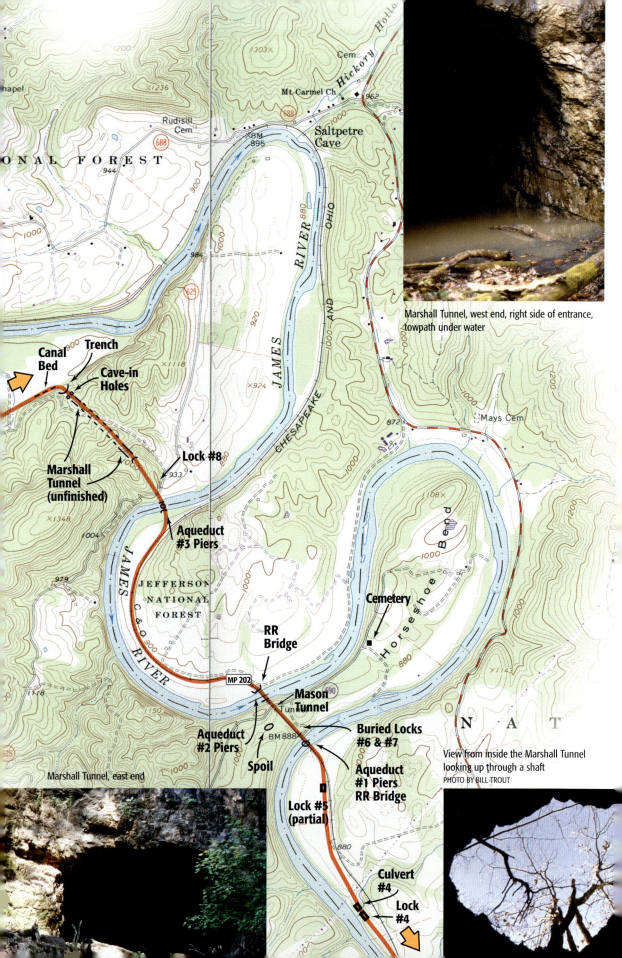

Marshall Tunnel, west end, right side of entrance, towpath under water

Marshall Tunnel, east end

View from inside the Marshall Tunnel looking up through a shaft
PHOTO BY BILL TROUT

Mason Tunnel, east end. The canal company made the tunnel but never used it. The railroad increased the height and used the aqueduct piers for their bridges at each end.

Lower end of culvert #4 was never covered and serves as a good example of culvert construction. See top of trunk below. See also diagram on page 24.

Richmond & Alleghany RR bridge. Mason Tunnel on right.

T. Gibson Hobbs IV at upper end of culvert #4 ca. 1992

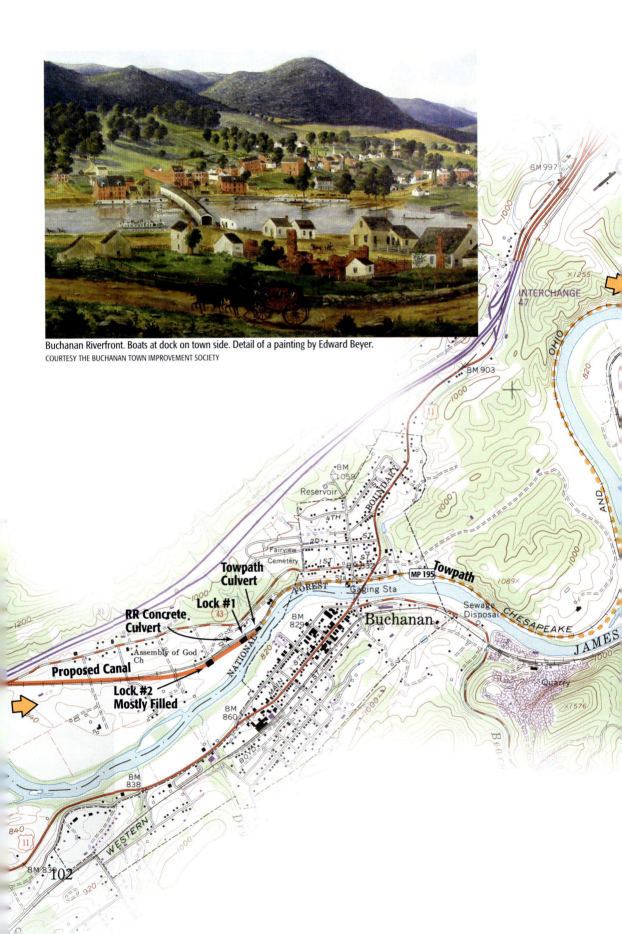

Buchanan Riverfront. Boats at dock on town side. Detail of a painting by Edward Beyer.
COURTESY THE BUCHANAN TOWN IMPROVEMENT SOCIETY

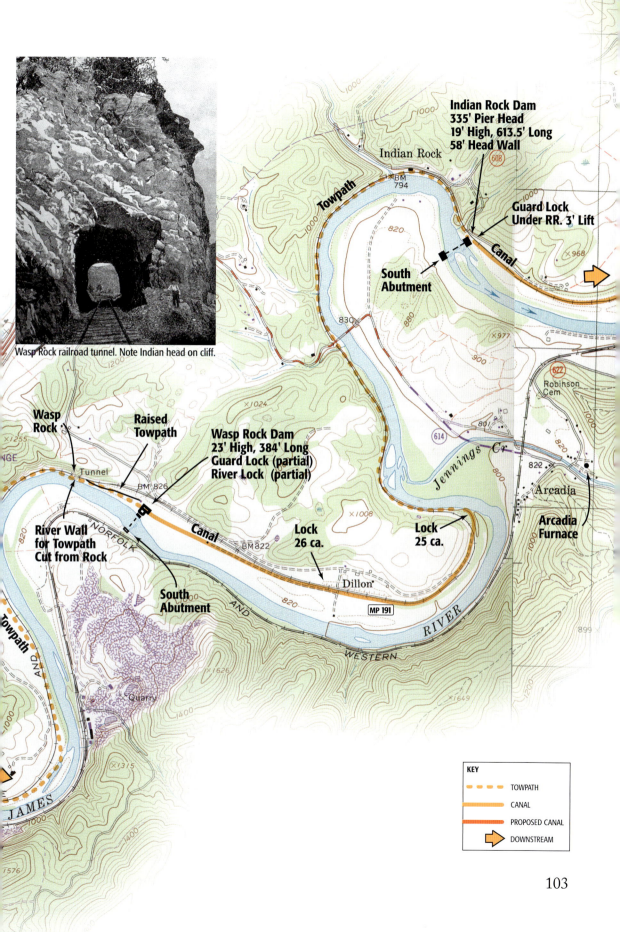

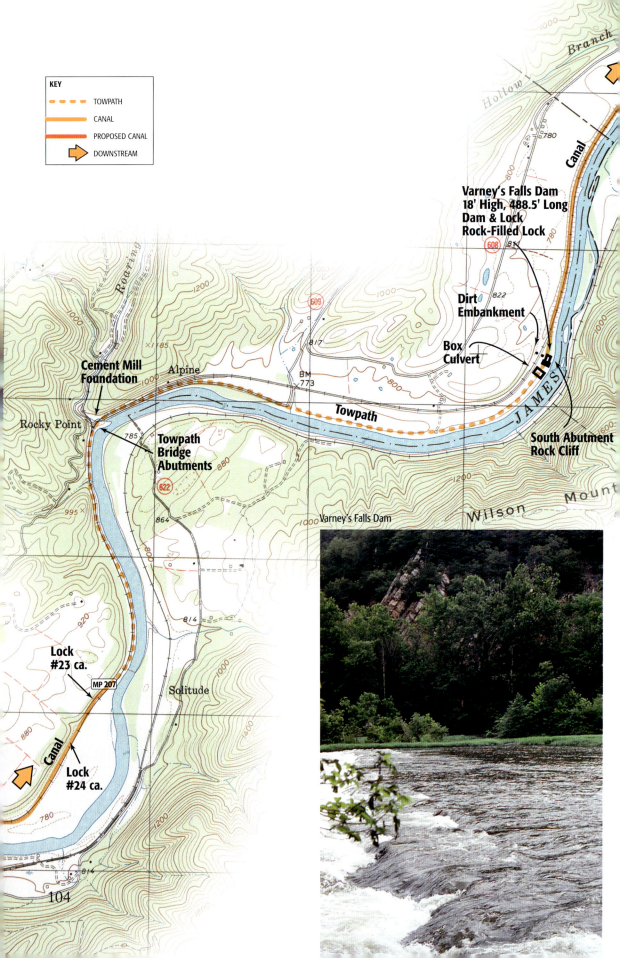

Timbers of Quarry Falls wooden dam

South abutment of Quarry Falls wooden dam

106

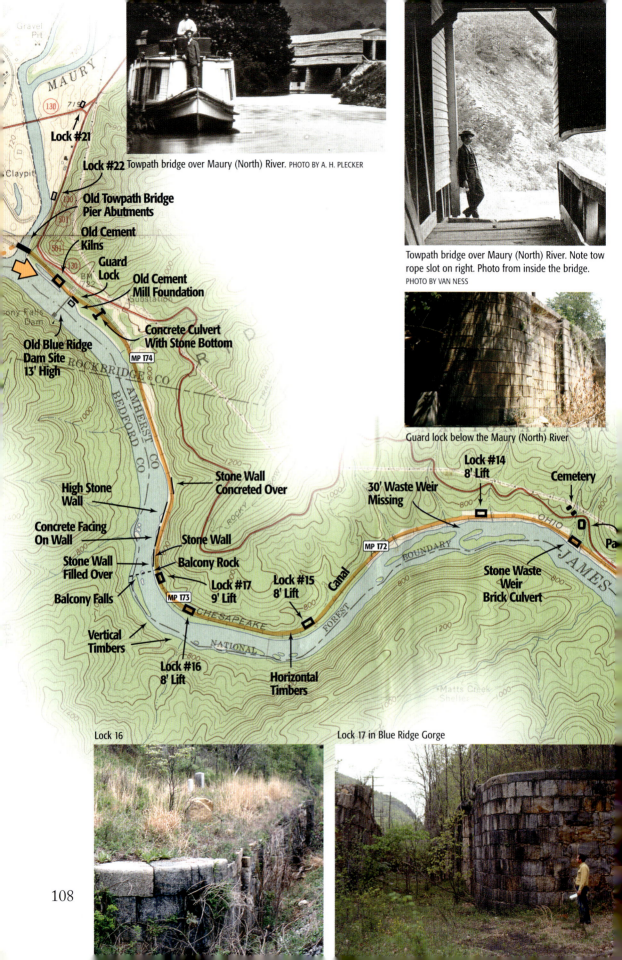

Cement Mill below Maury (North) River. PHOTO BY A. H. PLECKER

Lock 17, ca. 1900. PHOTO BY A. H. PLECKER

Blue Ridge Dam guard lock

Blue Ridge cement plant and lock from below

Blue Ridge Dam lock wall

Blue Ridge Dam and cement plant

Remains of Balcony Falls Dam

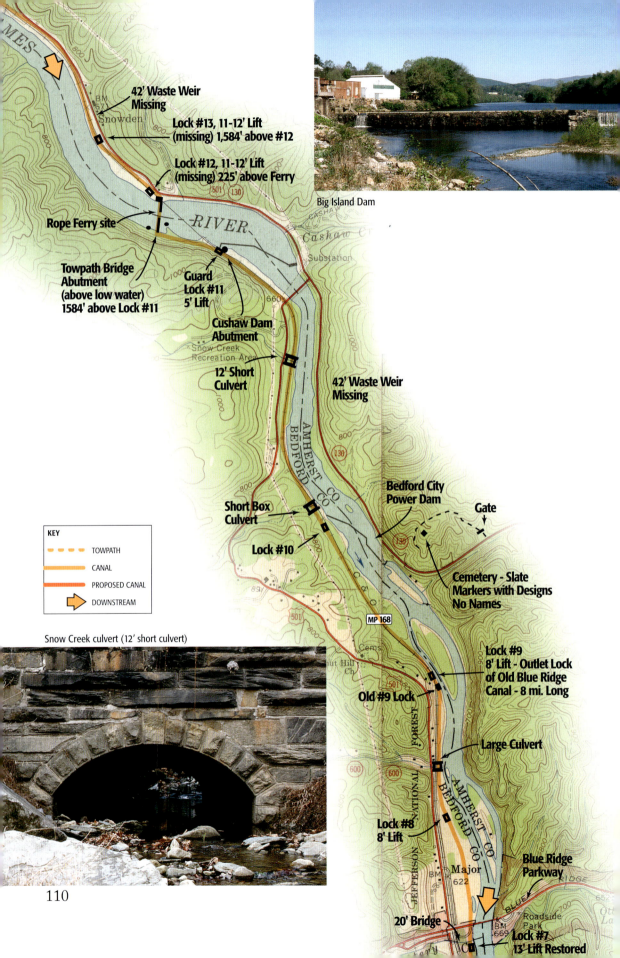

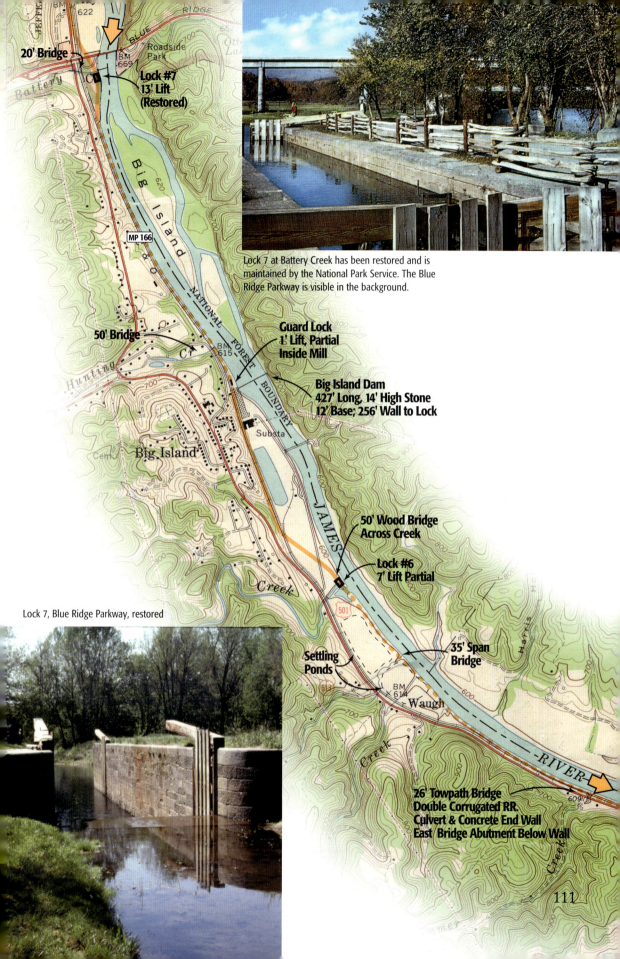

Richmond & Alleghany RR near Coleman Falls below Big Island. Note lock and Lock House No. 5.

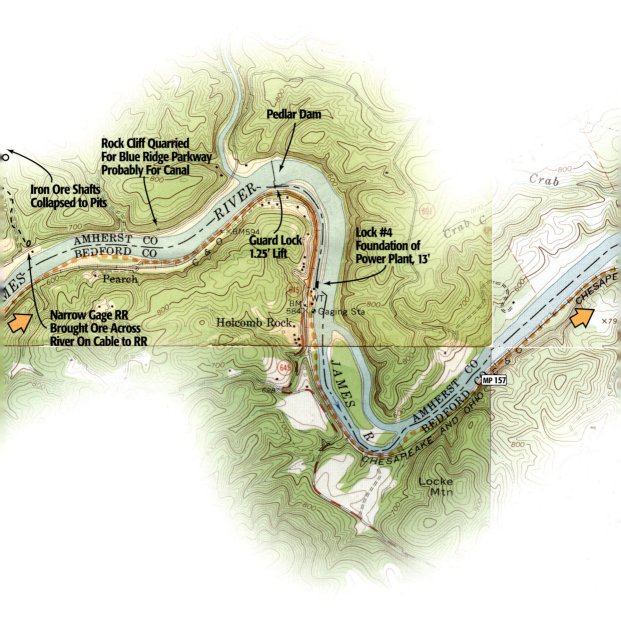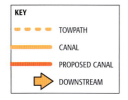

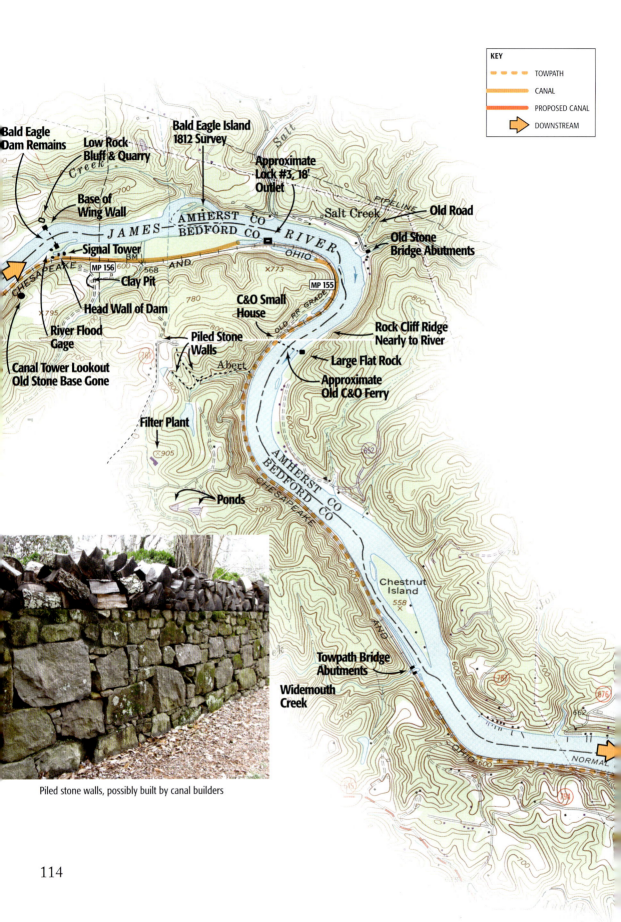

Piled stone walls, possibly built by canal builders

114

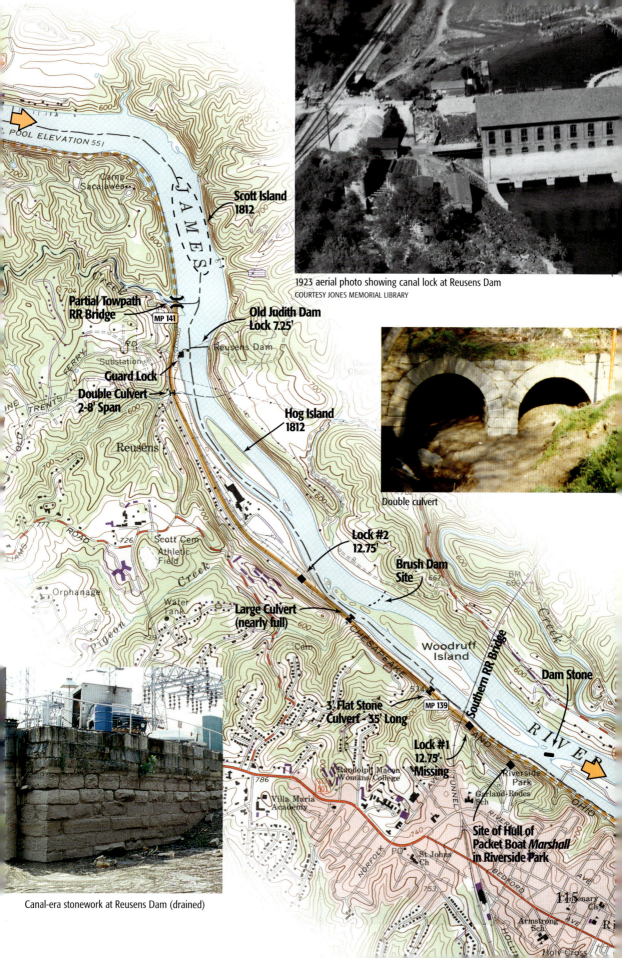

1923 aerial photo showing canal lock at Reusens Dam
COURTESY JONES MEMORIAL LIBRARY

Double culvert

Canal-era stonework at Reusens Dam (drained)

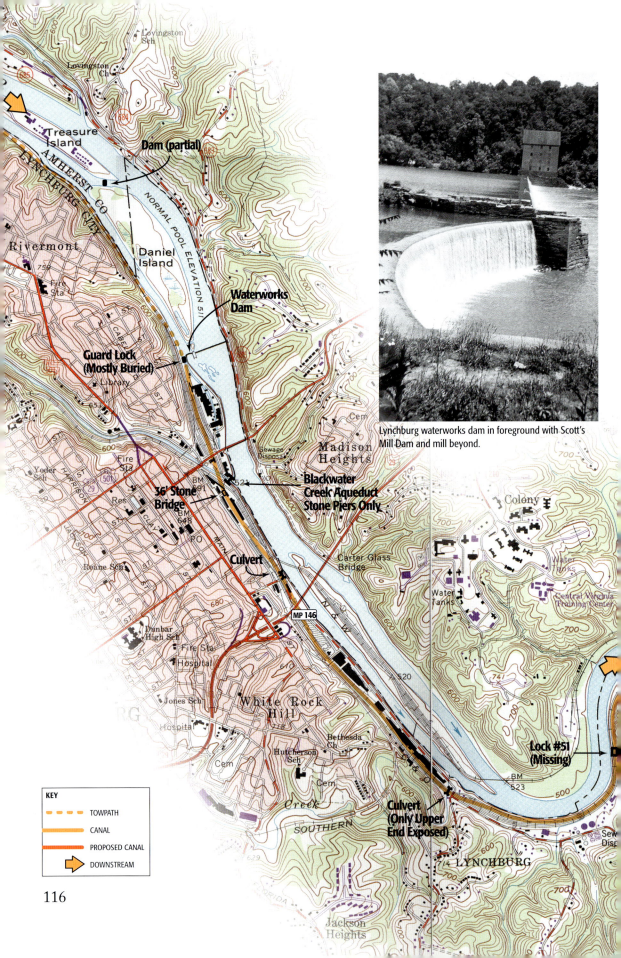

Lynchburg waterworks dam in foreground with Scott's Mill Dam and mill beyond.

Canal as it still existed wedged between the N&W freight warehouse on right and the C&O trains on the left. View is from about 11th Street.
COURTESY CHESAPEAKE AND OHIO HISTORICAL SOCIETY

9th Street stone arch bridge over canal. Bed now filled in. Bridge led to old covered bridge over James River.
PHOTO BY NANCY MARION

See more images of the canal in Lynchburg on pages 50–65.

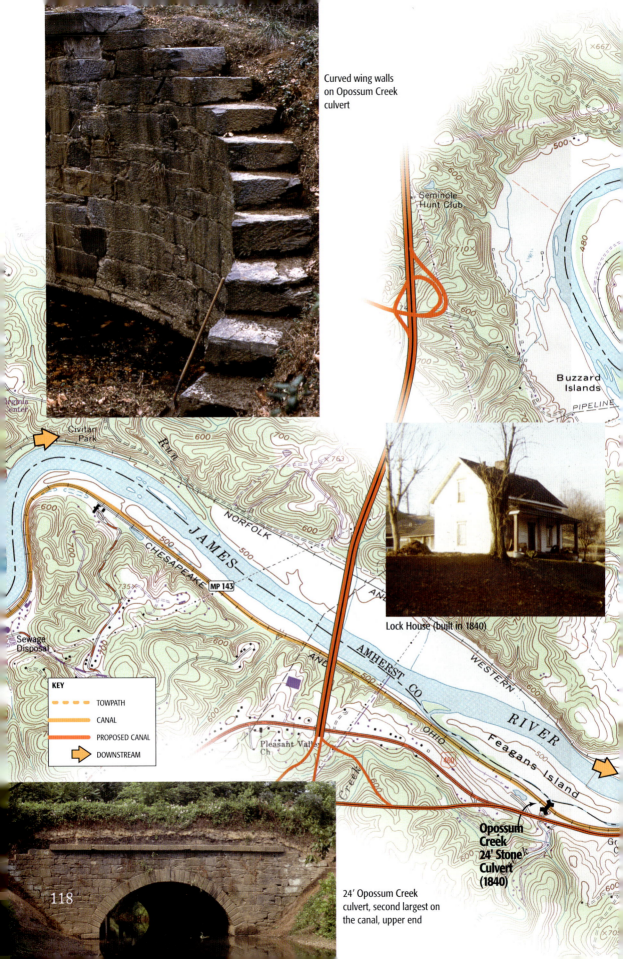

Curved wing walls on Opossum Creek culvert

Lock House (built in 1840)

KEY
- - - TOWPATH
——— CANAL
——— PROPOSED CANAL
➔ DOWNSTREAM

Opossum Creek 24' Stone Culvert (1840)

24' Opossum Creek culvert, second largest on the canal, upper end

118

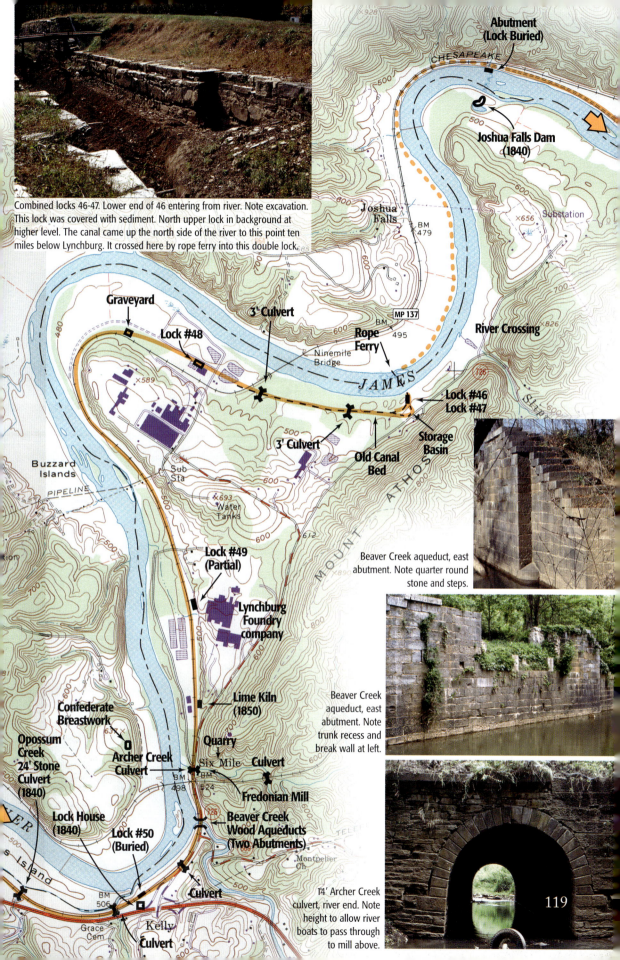

Towpath (left) and canal bed (right) above locks 46–47. This is one of the few places where the railroad does not run on the old towpath.

Lock 46, lower gate recess on south side. Closeup of wood with nails and bolt.

Lock 47, upper lock with steps up. North side, note middle gate.

Lock 46, looking along north side. Coping stone on top.

Left: 3' culvert above locks 46–47. Note angled wing walls.

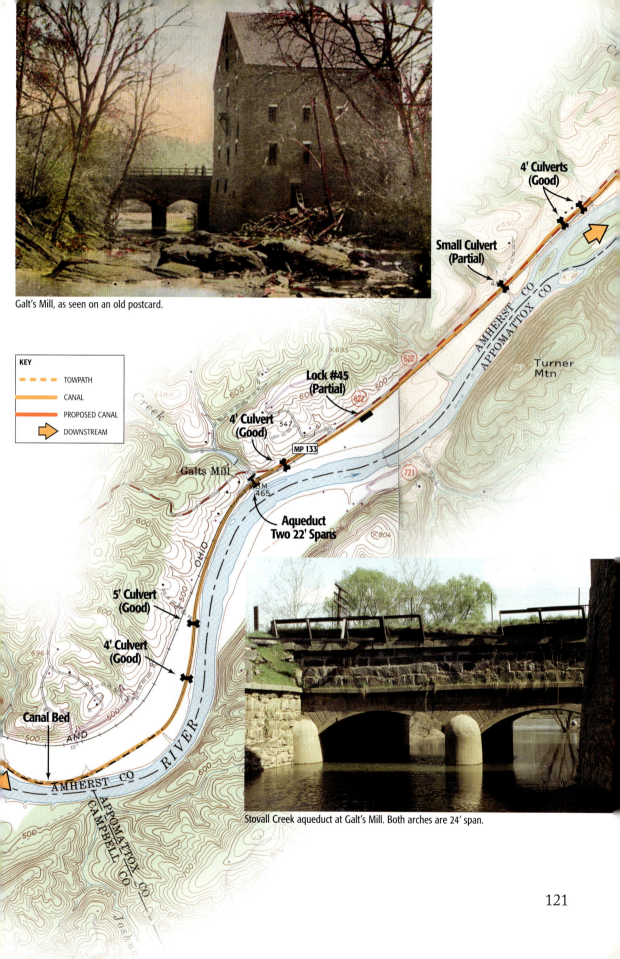

Galt's Mill, as seen on an old postcard.

Stovall Creek aqueduct at Galt's Mill. Both arches are 24' span.

T. Gibson Hobbs IV at 15' Pudding Hill culvert

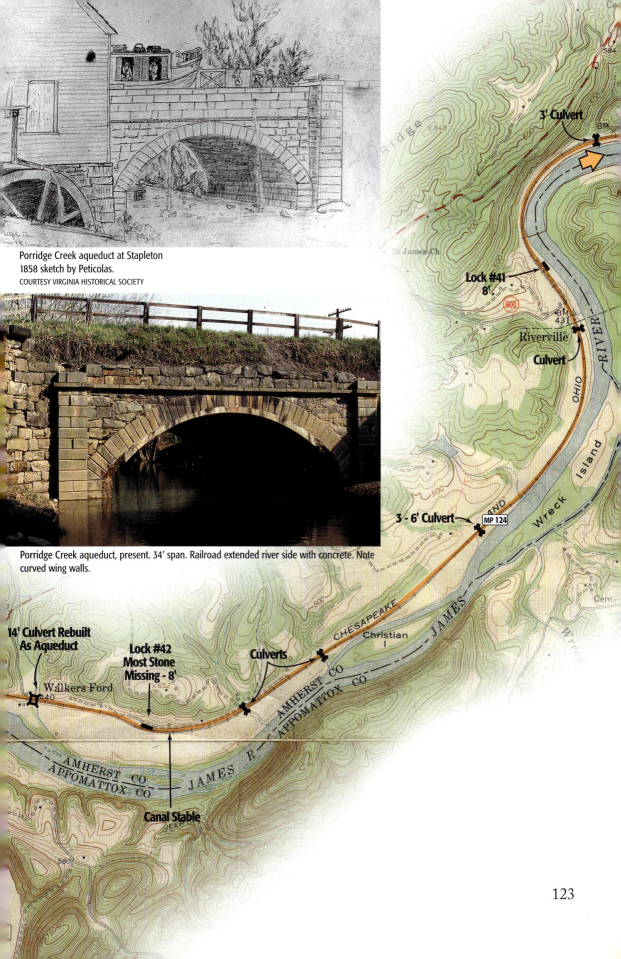

Porridge Creek aqueduct at Stapleton
1858 sketch by Peticolas.
COURTESY VIRGINIA HISTORICAL SOCIETY

Porridge Creek aqueduct, present. 34' span. Railroad extended river side with concrete. Note curved wing walls.

123

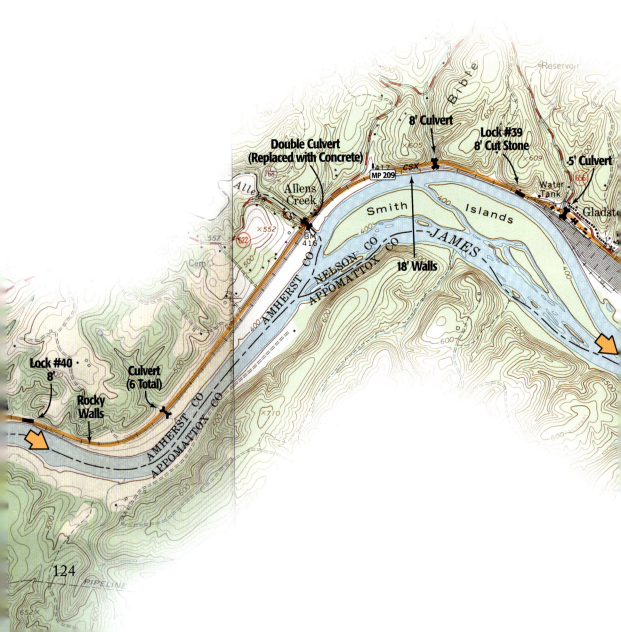

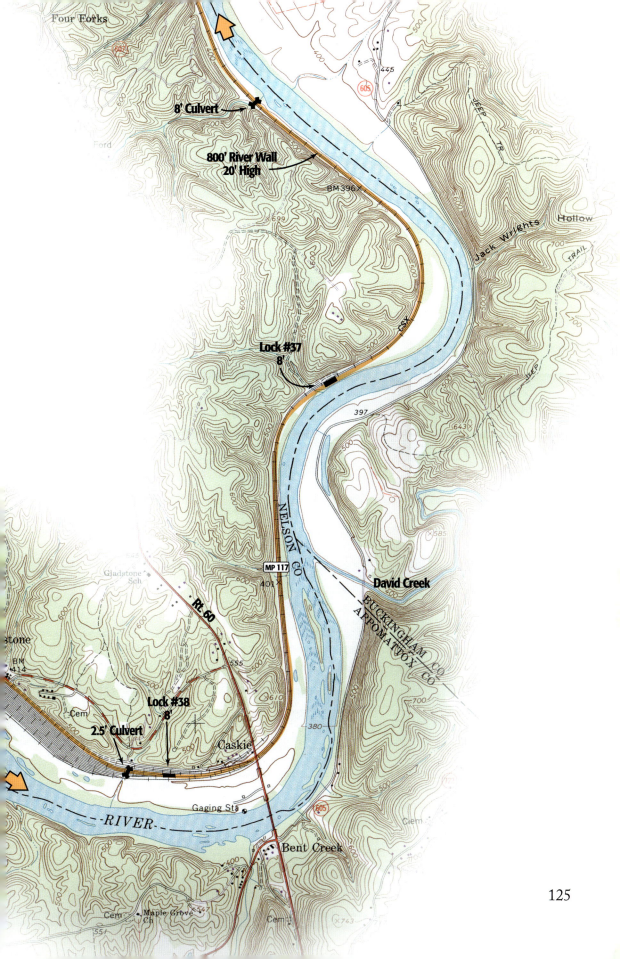

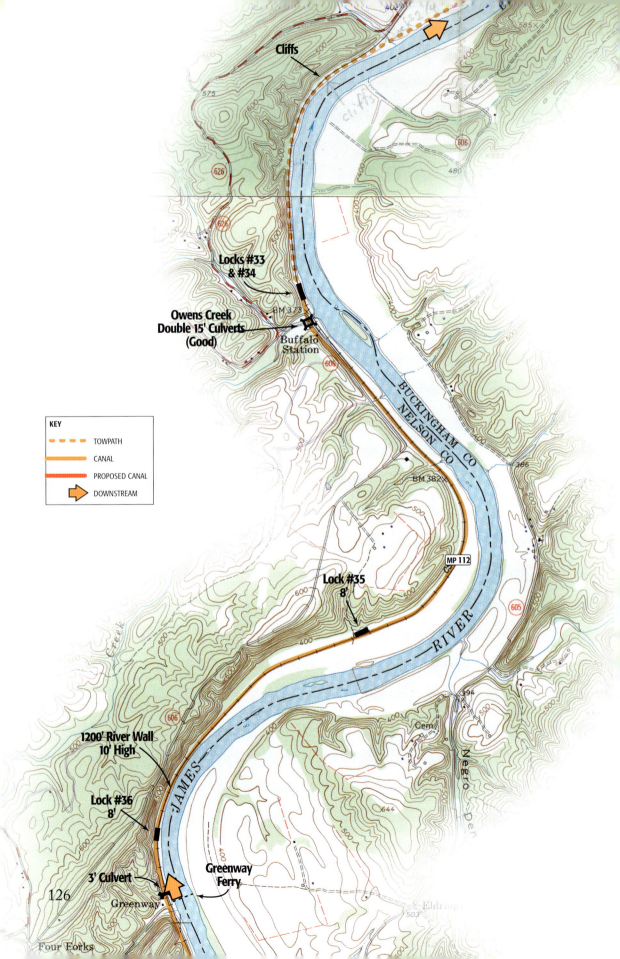

Owens Creek culvert, upper end. Double 15' culverts. River side of this culvert has been extended in concrete by the railroad.

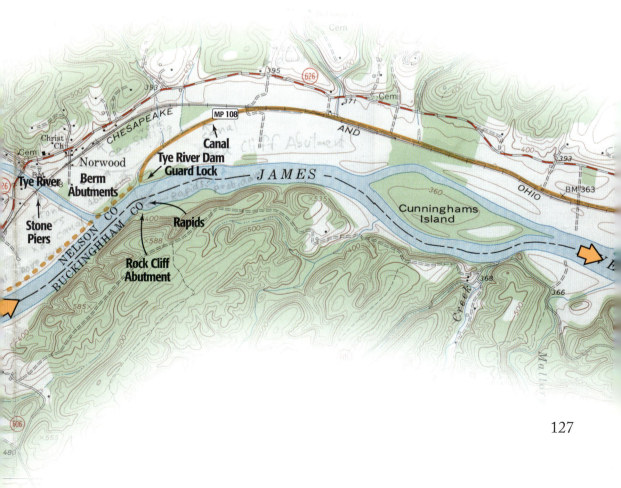

Culvert at Midway Mills, Nelson County, 1989

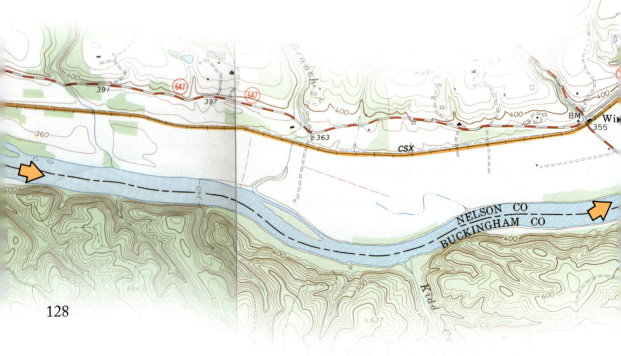

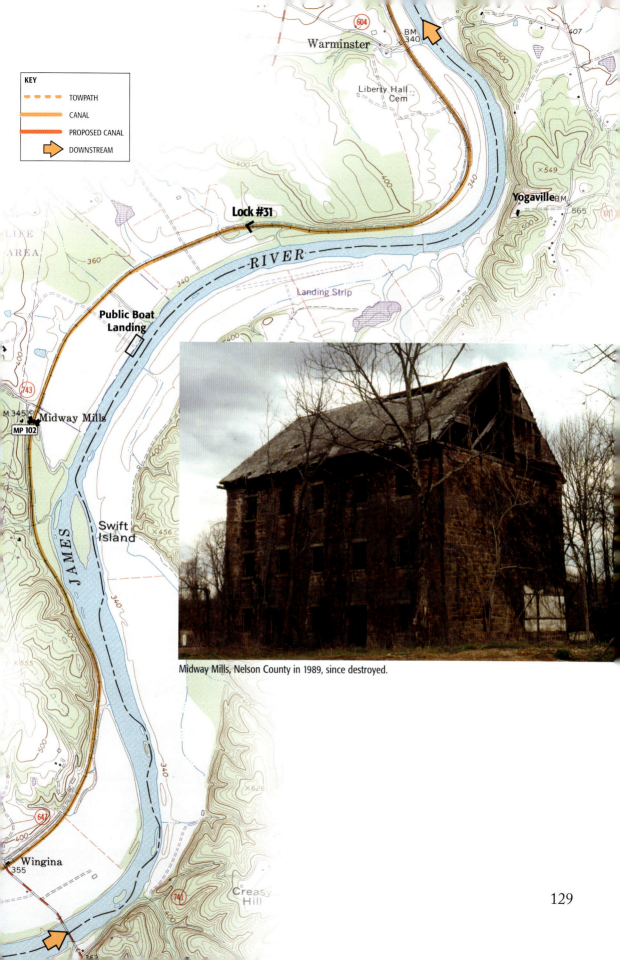

Midway Mills, Nelson County in 1989, since destroyed.

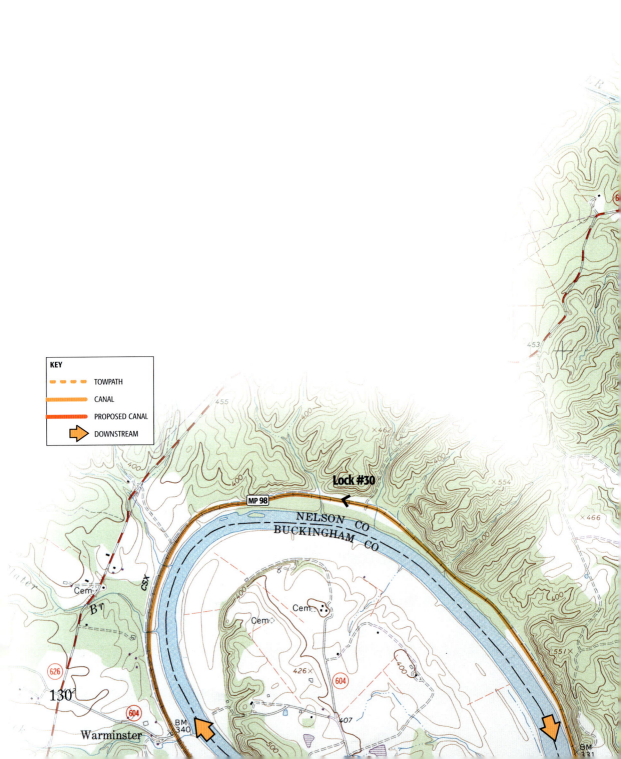

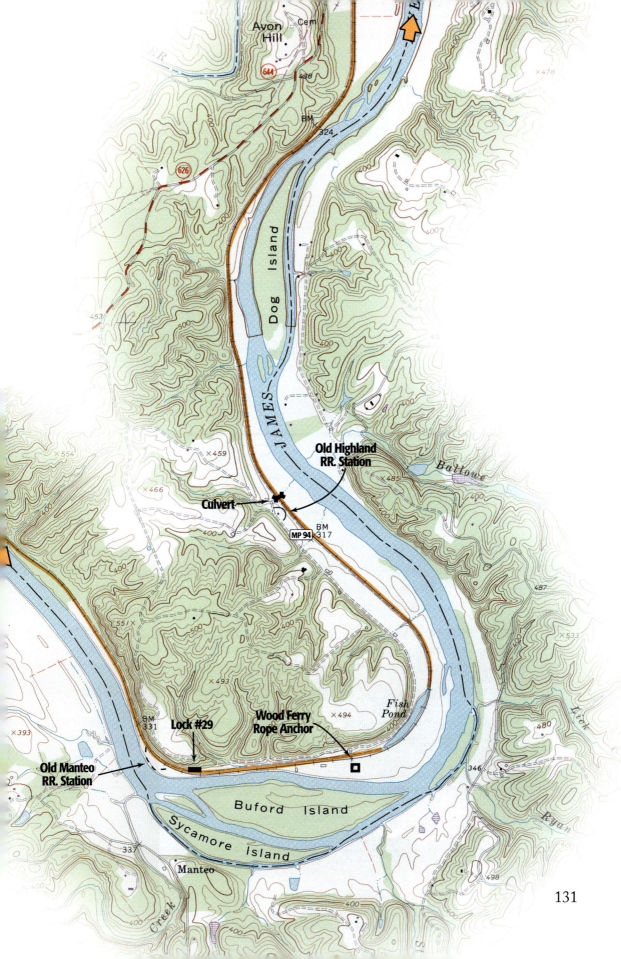

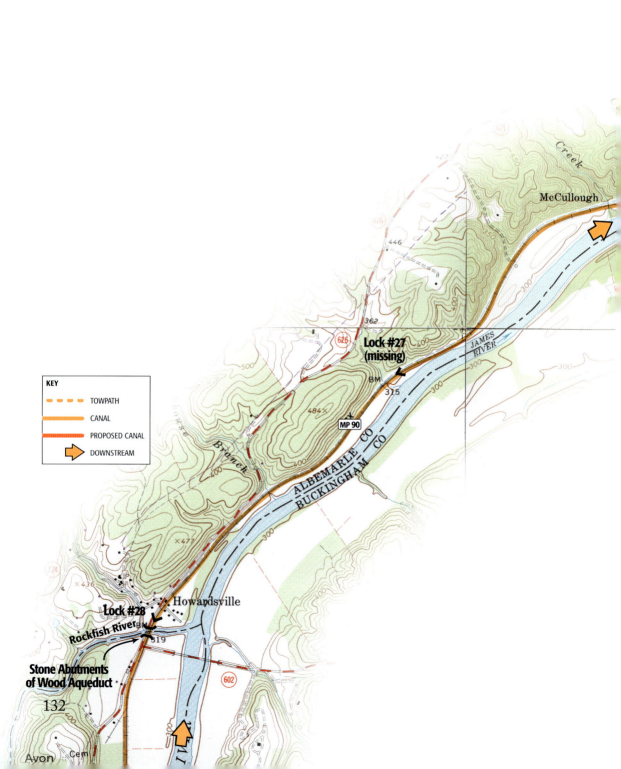

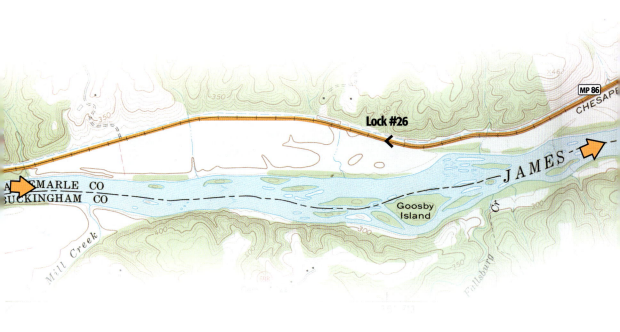

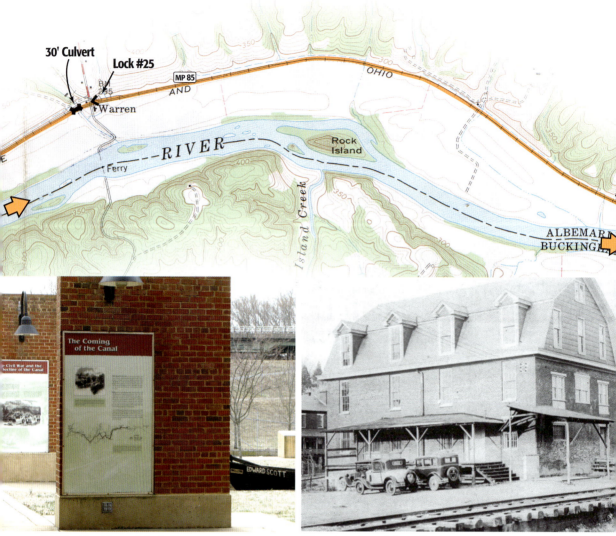

134　Hatton Ferry, circa 1910, from the Buckingham County shore.
PHOTO COURTESY THE SCOTTSVILLE MUSEUM AND VIRGINIA CANALS AND NAVIGATIONS SOCIETY

Exhibits at Canal Square in Scottsville

Old canal warehouse in Scottsville circa 1925
PHOTO BY WILLIAM E. BURGESS, COURTESY THE SCOTTSVILLE MUSEUM AND VIRGINIA CANALS AND NAVIGATIONS SOCIETY

Hatton Ferry is one of two pole-operated ferries still existing in the U.S. This photo from 1972 shows Ned Hockett who operated it for many years.
PHOTO BY BILL TROUT

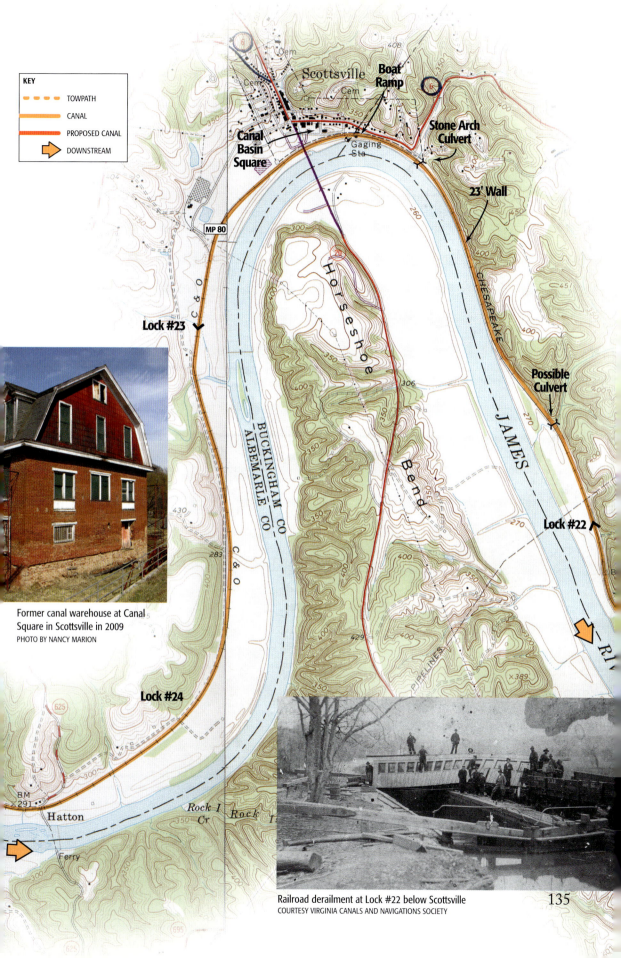

Former canal warehouse at Canal Square in Scottsville in 2009
PHOTO BY NANCY MARION

Railroad derailment at Lock #22 below Scottsville
COURTESY VIRGINIA CANALS AND NAVIGATIONS SOCIETY

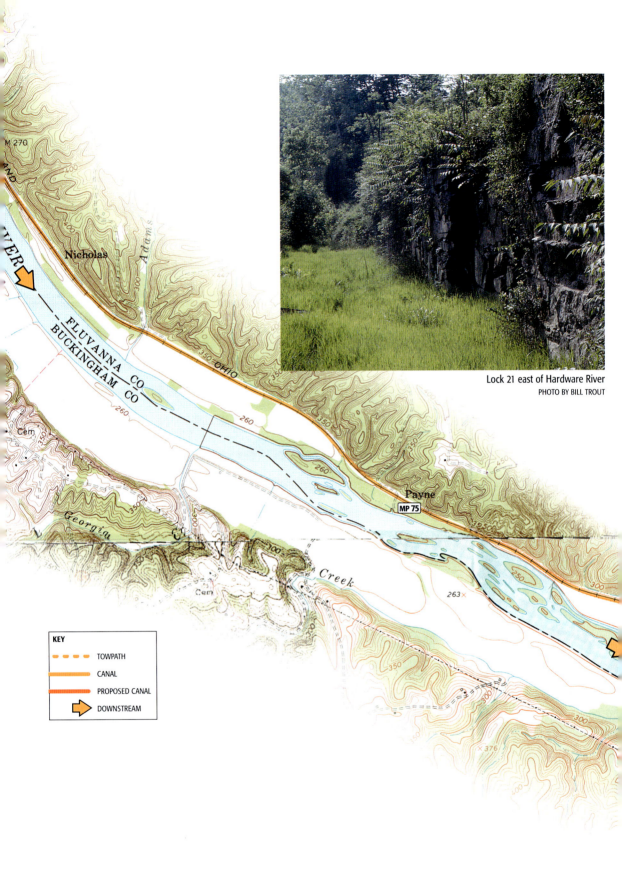

Lock 21 east of Hardware River
PHOTO BY BILL TROUT

KEY
- - - - TOWPATH
━━━━ CANAL
━━━━ PROPOSED CANAL
➡ DOWNSTREAM

Mason's mark on Hardware aqueduct
PHOTO BY BILL TROUT

Hardware aqueduct

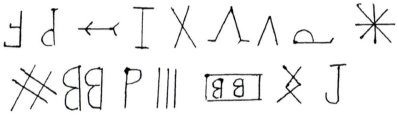

Mason's marks recorded by Bill Trout on the Hardware River aqueduct.
COURTESY THE VIRGINIA CANALS AND NAVIGATIONS SOCIETY

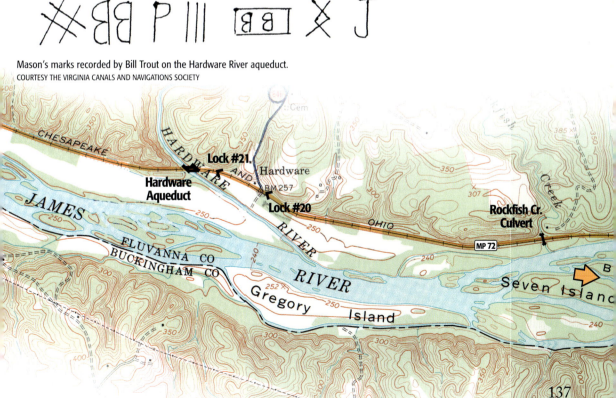

Little Bremo Creek culvert, 1 mi. west of Cocke Bridge, Bremo
PHOTO BY BILL TROUT

Big Bremo Creek culvert
PHOTO BY BILL TROUT

Culvert at power company east of Bremo
PHOTO BY BILL TROUT

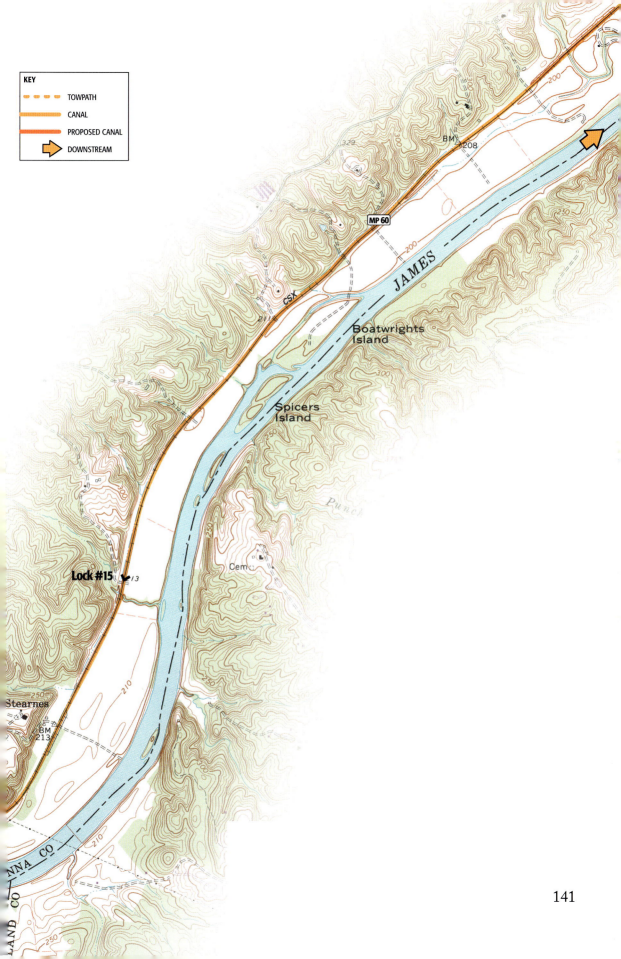

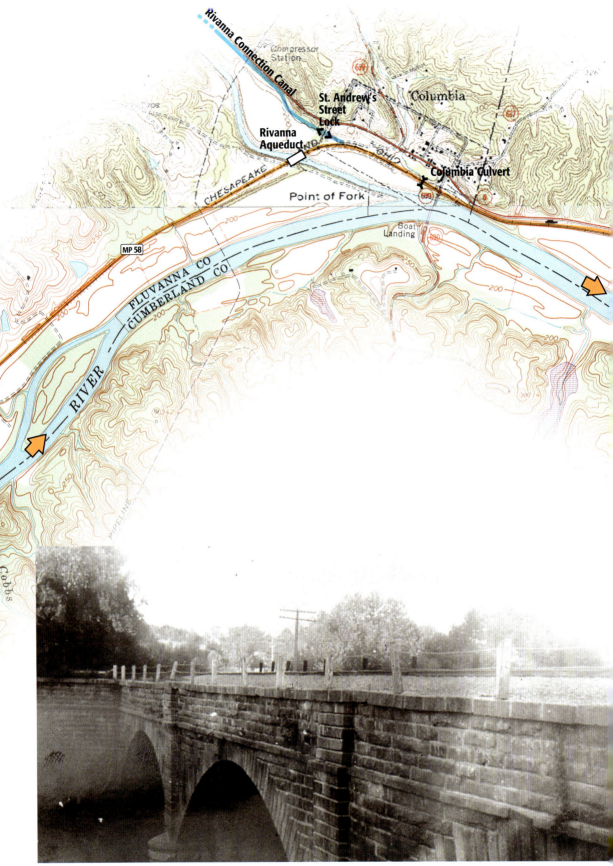

Rivanna River aqueduct, demolished in the 1940s.
PHOTO COURTESY BILL TROUT

Remains of Rivanna River aqueduct
PHOTO BY BILL TROUT

143

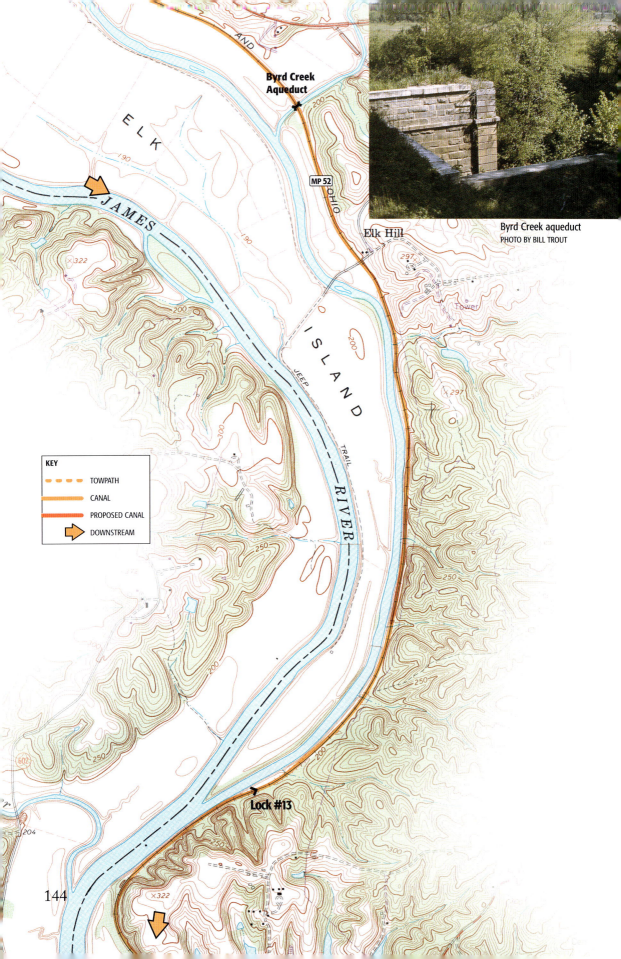

Byrd Creek aqueduct
PHOTO BY BILL TROUT

144

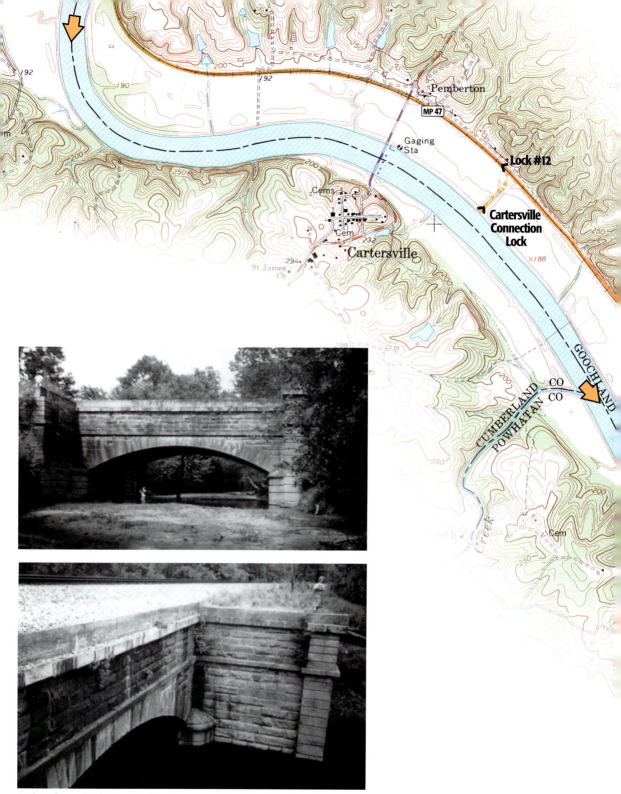

Byrd Creek aqueduct in Goochland County now carries trains instead of canal boats. See drawing on page 8.
PHOTO ABOVE BY LYNN HOWLETT. TOP PHOTO BY MINNIE LEE MCGEHEE, COURTESY THE VIRGINIA CANALS AND NAVIGATIONS SOCIETY

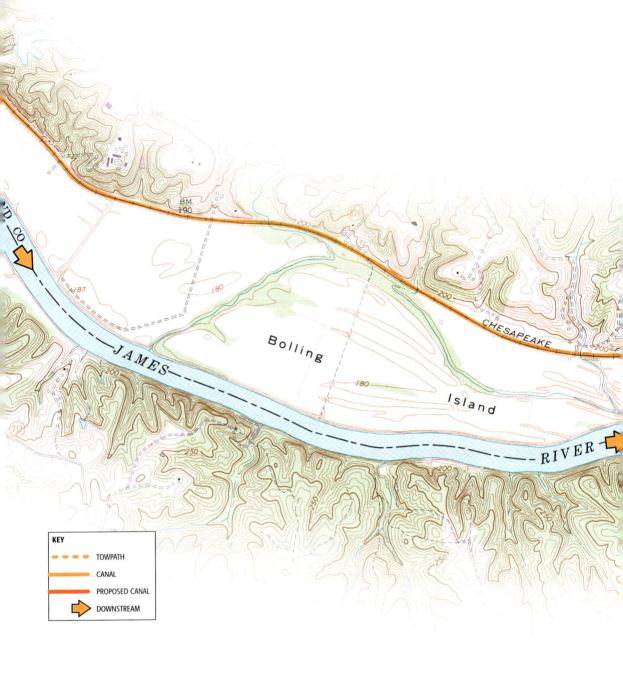

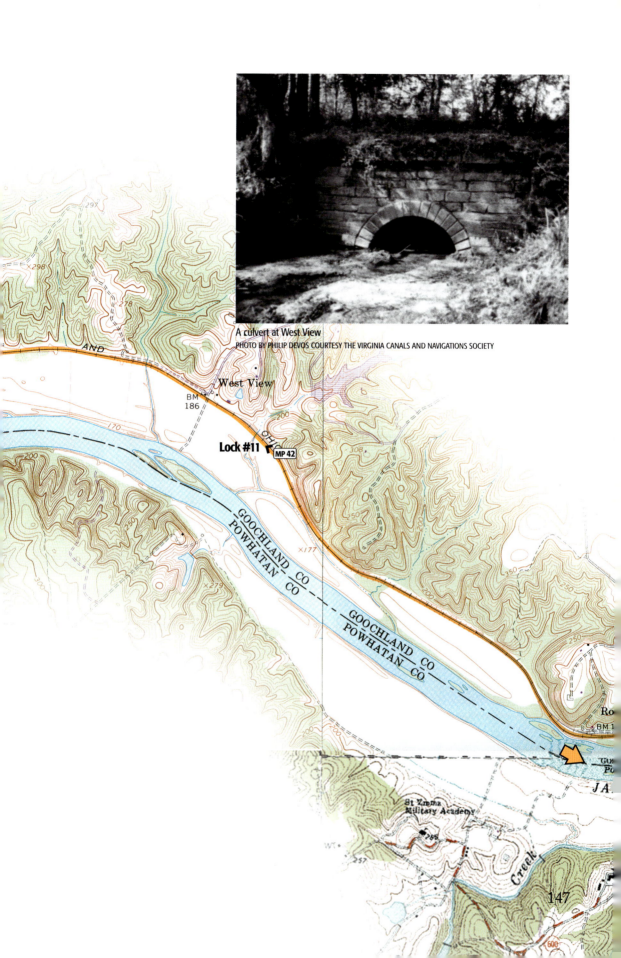

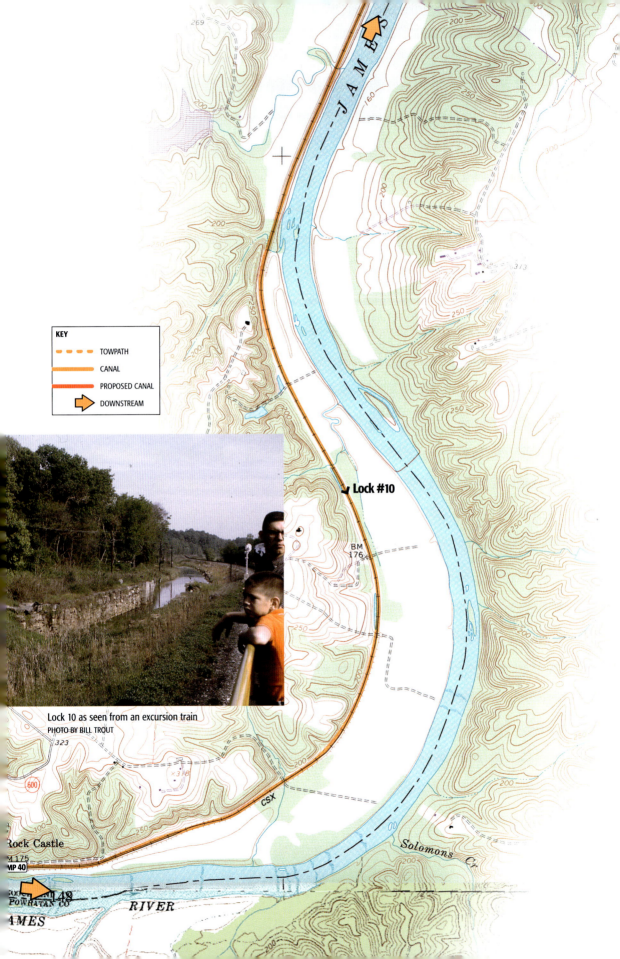

Lock 10 as seen from an excursion train
PHOTO BY BILL TROUT

Arrow on Licking Hole Creek aqueduct
PHOTO BY BILL TROUT

Licking Hole Creek aqueduct
PHOTO BY BILL TROUT

Little Creek Culvert 20-foot stone arch one of the largest on the canal

Licking Hole Creek Aqueduct Lock #9

Cedar Point Lock #8

Lock #7

The white stone lockhouse at Cedar Point is visible from the river. Here Locks 7 and 8 lowered canal boats into the river. They were towed for five miles from a towpath along the riverbank, down to the lock in Maiden's Adventure Dam.

Cedar Point lockkeeper's house
PHOTO BY LYNN HOWLETT COURTESY THE VIRGINIA CANALS AND NAVIGATIONS SOCIETY

Licking Hole Creek aqueduct
PHOTO BY PHILIP DEVOS COURTESY THE VIRGINIA CANALS AND NAVIGATIONS SOCIETY

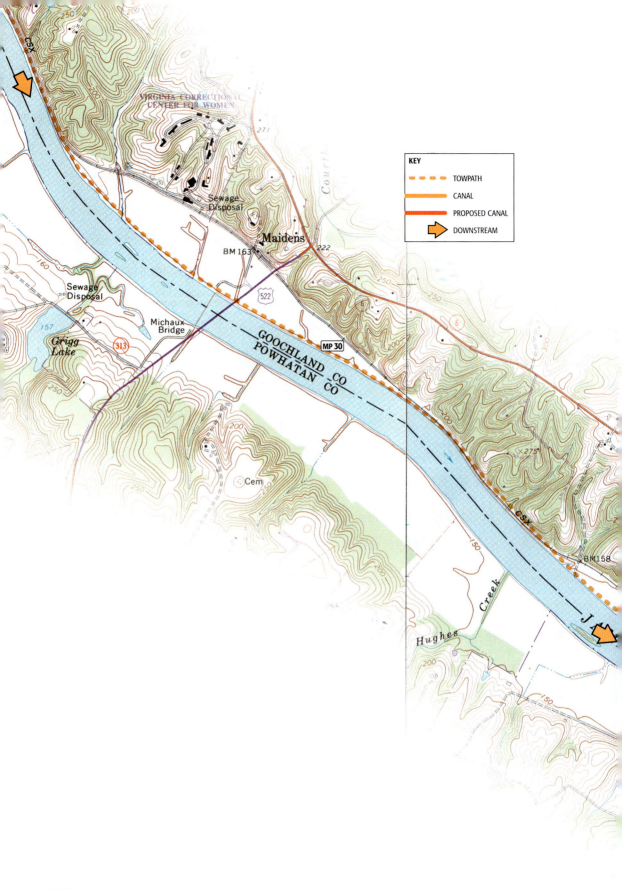

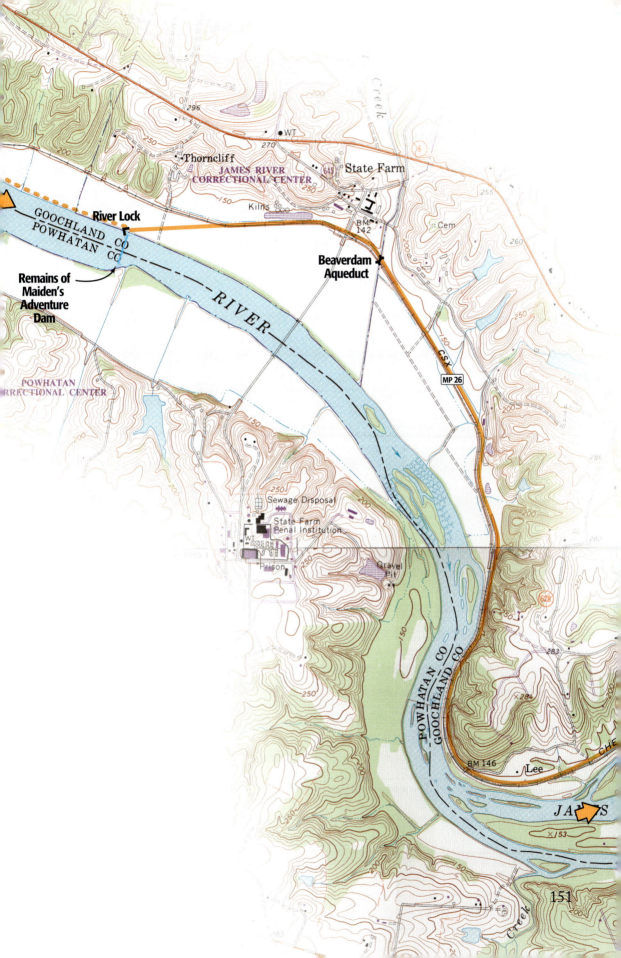

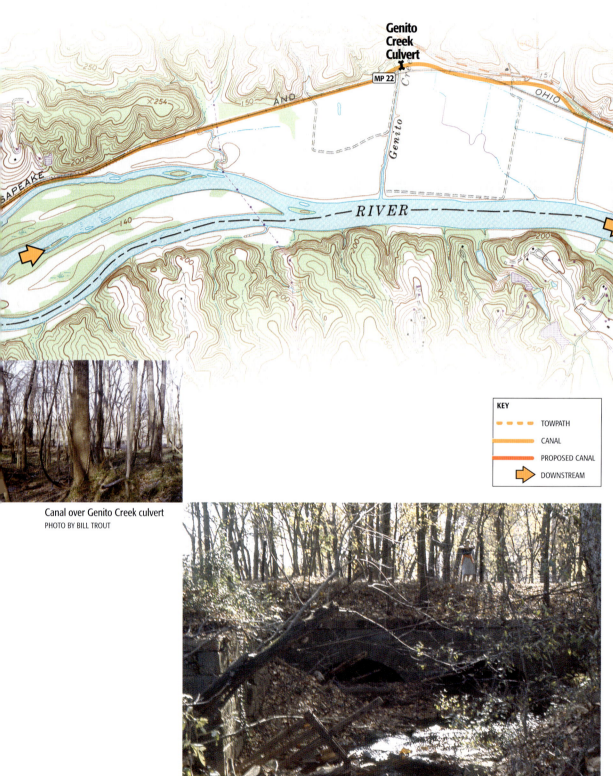

Canal over Genito Creek culvert
PHOTO BY BILL TROUT

Double-arched Genito Creek culvert, north end
PHOTO BY BILL TROUT

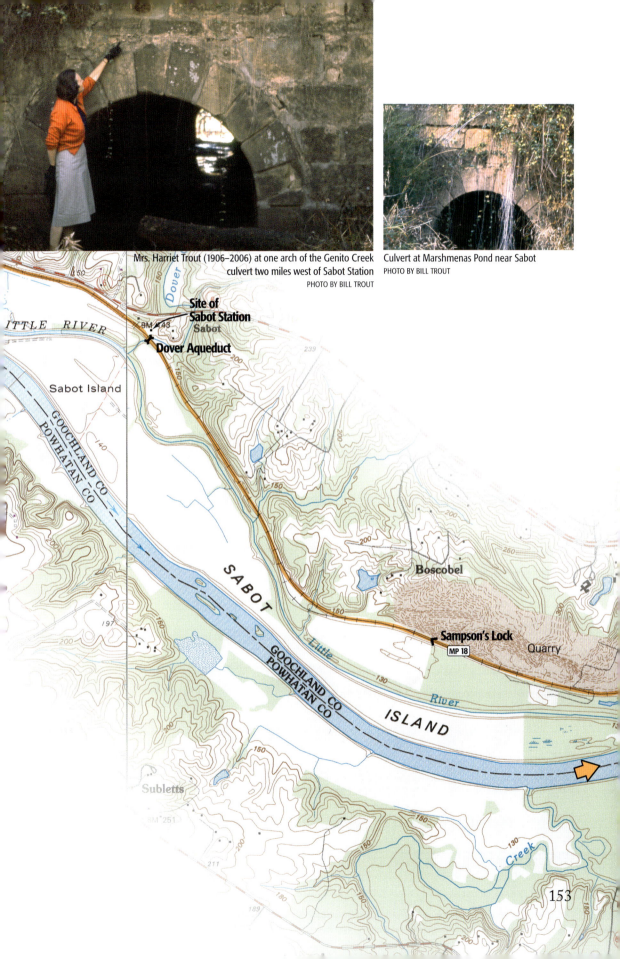

Mrs. Harriet Trout (1906–2006) at one arch of the Genito Creek culvert two miles west of Sabot Station
PHOTO BY BILL TROUT

Culvert at Marshmenas Pond near Sabot
PHOTO BY BILL TROUT

Packet boats near the mouth of Tuckahoe Creek ca. 1881.

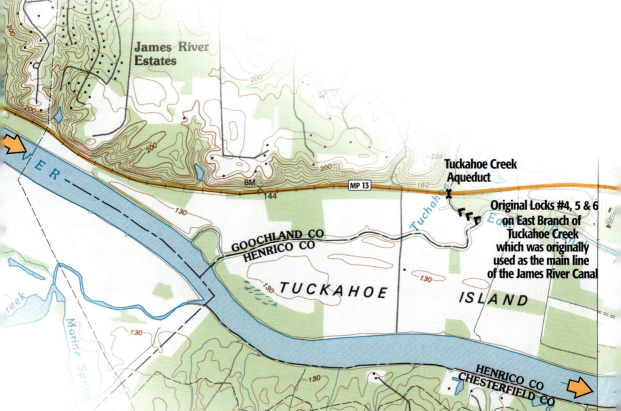

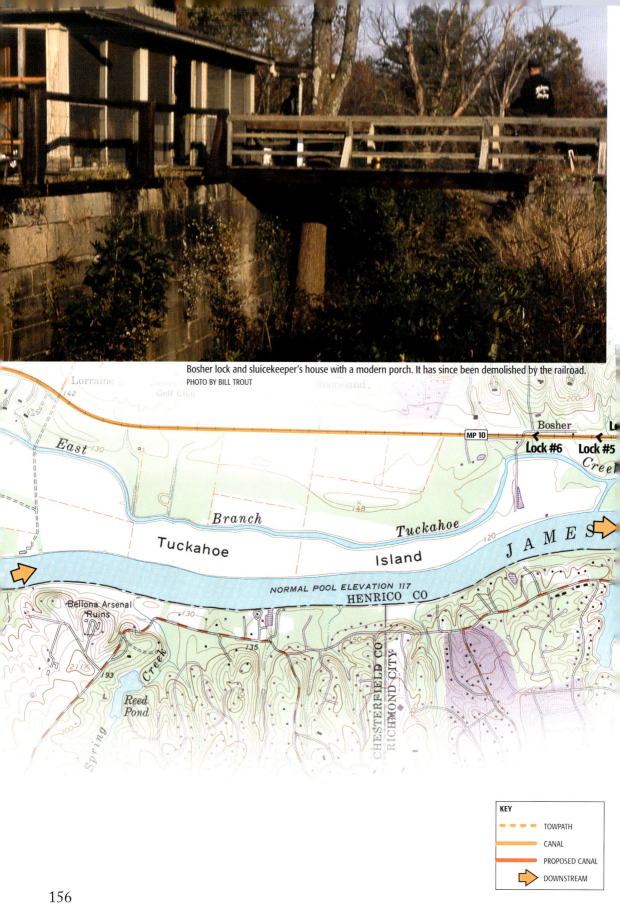

Bosher lock and sluicekeeper's house with a modern porch. It has since been demolished by the railroad.
PHOTO BY BILL TROUT

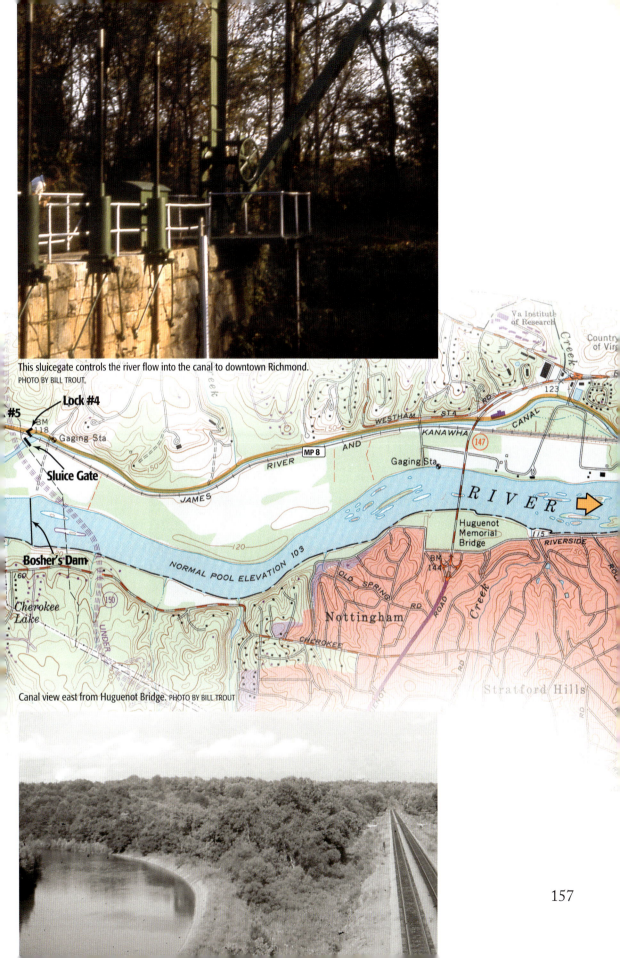

This sluicegate controls the river flow into the canal to downtown Richmond.
PHOTO BY BILL TROUT

Canal view east from Huguenot Bridge. PHOTO BY BILL TROUT

157

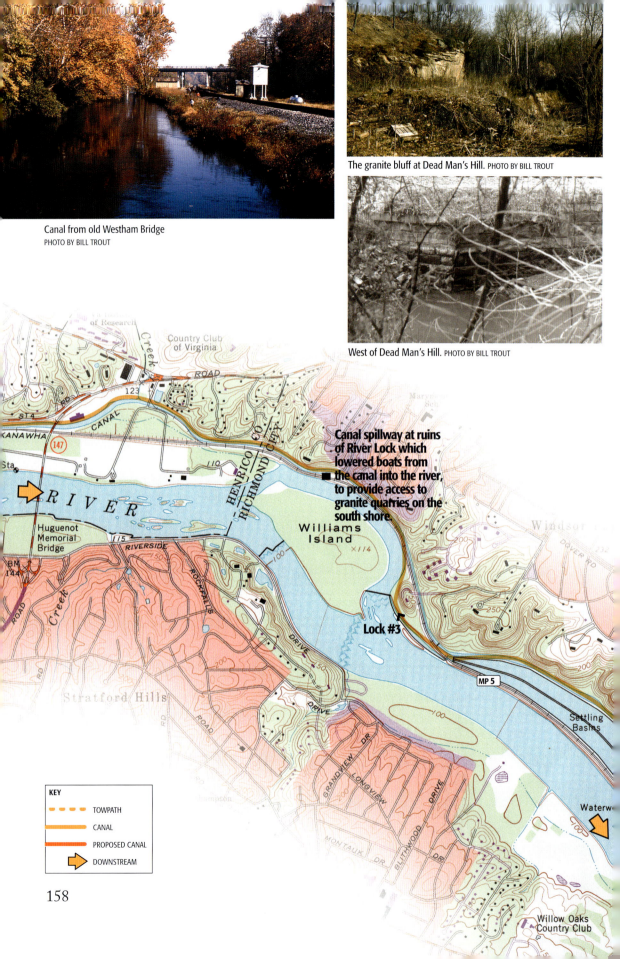

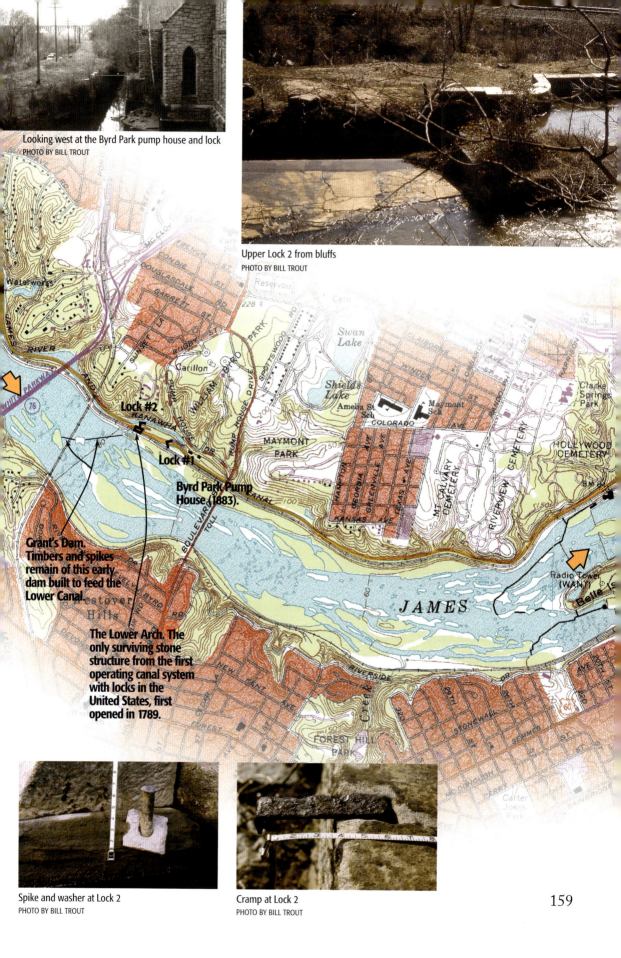

Looking west at the Byrd Park pump house and lock
PHOTO BY BILL TROUT

Upper Lock 2 from bluffs
PHOTO BY BILL TROUT

Lock #2

Lock #1

Byrd Park Pump House (1883).

Grant's Dam. Timbers and spikes remain of this early dam built to feed the Lower Canal.

The Lower Arch. The only surviving stone structure from the first operating canal system with locks in the United States, first opened in 1789.

Spike and washer at Lock 2
PHOTO BY BILL TROUT

Cramp at Lock 2
PHOTO BY BILL TROUT

The canal in downtown Richmond has been redeveloped into a tourist mecca with canal boat rides and a historic "canal walk."

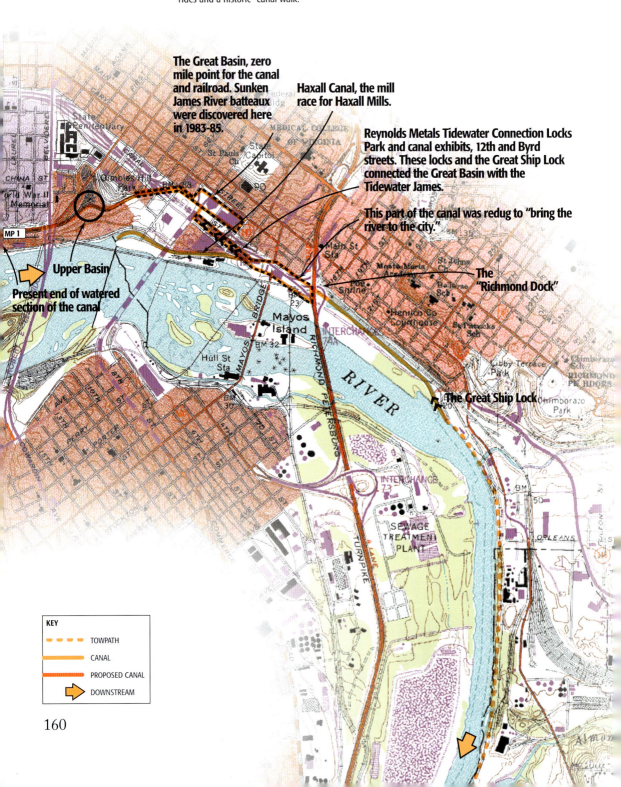

Tidewater Connection. Upper gate recess and coping

Tidewater Connection. Lower lock from upper end. Bridge in distance.

Ship Lock, lower gates. Ships from river lifted up to one-mile-long dock in lower Richmond.

Tidewater Connection. Upper lock, looking to lower lock.

Tidewater Connection. Lower gate recess of lower lock from bridge.

Tidewater Connection. Lower lock looking under 37th Street bridge toward ship dock.

Tidewater Connection. Lower lock, looking to upper lock.

Resources

Unless noted, all of the photographs used in this book are from the research collection of T. Gibson Hobbs, Jr. The collection, which includes his maps, papers, artifacts, and other research materials, is currently housed at the Jones Memorial Library and the Lynchburg Museum.

JONES MEMORIAL LIBRARY

The T. Gibson Hobbs, Jr. collection contains more than 3,000 slides. Most of these were taken between 1974 and 1991 by Gibson Hobbs as he and legions of his friends cleared trees and brush to uncover the neglected ruins of the canal. Some of the slides include images from books and other sources which recorded the people and places of the story. The USGS topographical maps on which he recorded the works of the canal are also included.

Gibson researched the construction of the canal using many primary sources such as minutes of stockholders' meetings, logs of surveyors from the Board of Public Works, and daybooks of the JR&KC. Photocopies of this material and, in some cases, the originals are part of his collection stored at the library.

His papers also include much genealogical research on such families as Imboden, Hobbs, and Bolling. Other topics in his files include mills and furnaces, waterworks, bridges, railroads, and the Civil War.

The Jones Memorial Library is located at 2311 Memorial Avenue, Lynchburg, VA. 434-846-0501. Hours of operation: Tuesday and Thursday 1:00–9:00 p.m., Wednesday and Friday 1:00–5:00 p.m., Saturday 9:00 a.m.–5:00 p.m. A more complete list of the holdings of the library is available online at JML.org under Catalogs.

THE LYNCHBURG MUSEUM

Gibson donated several canal-related artifacts to the Lynchburg Museum, such as nails, wood, and miscellaneous iron pieces of canal locks. The museum is at 901 Court Street, Lynchburg, VA. 434-455-6226. LynchburgMuseum.org

THE VIRGINIA CANALS AND NAVIGATIONS SOCIETY

Some photos and records of the society are housed at the archives of the Fluvanna Historical Society. Many others are in the personal collections of Minnie Lee McGehee in Palmyra and Bill Trout in Edenton, NC. The official records of the society are archived at the Library of Virginia. A listing is available online at lva.virginia.gov. The web site for the VCNS is vacanals.org.

For a current list of resources, visit BlackwellPress.net/canal.

Relive the Canal

Along the old route of the canal, several special places commemorate its former glory. The list below highlights the best places to witness this history for yourself.

RICHMOND CANAL BASIN

This award-winning transformation of a two-mile-long corridor came to life when a combined sewer overflow installation resulted in the unearthing of a historic canal. Improvements include canal walls, walkways, terraces, pedestrian bridges, and steps and ramps to provide access to the canal from street level. Pedestrian plazas are at the east end of the Haxall Canal and Turning Basin. Canal cruises offer an informative 40-minute historically narrated tour or private charter of the James River and Kanawha Canal along Richmond's Historic Canal Walk.

SCOTTSVILLE'S CANAL BASIN SQUARE

To learn about Scottsville's river history, visit the outdoor exhibit at Canal Basin Square (249 E. Main St., 434-286-9267). The ca. 1840 Canal Warehouse still stands adjacent to the square. Stroll the Levee Walk and explore the historic district (maps are available at Canal Basin Square). The Scottsville Museum (290 Main St., 434-286-2247) is open Saturdays and Sundays, April through October.

AMAZEMENT SQUARE IN LYNCHBURG

(Rightmire Children's Museum) The "On the James" exhibit introduces visitors to the force and energy of moving water and the navigation challenges of taking a miniature bateau down the James while manipulating locks. At the "Board a Bateau" exhibit children pretend to be on a bateau in the 19th century wearing period costumes and experiencing the history of the region. Open Tuesday–Saturday, 10–5; Sunday, 1–5; Closed Monday except Memorial Day–Labor Day, 1–5. 27 Ninth Street, Lynchburg, VA. 434-845-1888. www.AmazementSquare.com

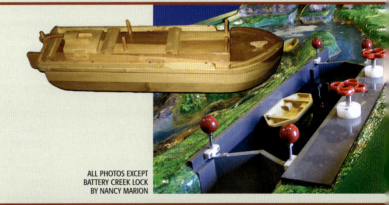

ALL PHOTOS EXCEPT BATTERY CREEK LOCK BY NANCY MARION

BATTERY CREEK LOCK

This park on the Blue Ridge Parkway at the James River displays a fully restored lock. The Canal Lock Trail (0.4 miles) begins at the Visitor Center and crosses the James River on a walk-way built beneath the bridge. Battery Creek Lock is located a short distance from the bridge. Exhibits at the Battery Creek site explain how locks were used to raise and lower boats to adjust for the changing elevation of the river. www.nps.gov/blri

Index

A
Abert, Colonel 38
Afton 42
Albany, New York 6
Alexander, Andrew 5
Alleghany Mountains 1, 2, 4, 5, 7, 22, 49, 66
American Society of Civil Engineers 32
Amherst County 25, 26, 55, 63
Appalachian Mountains 4, 41
Aqueduct construction 24
Archer Creek 15, 119
Army Corps of Engineers 6, 22, 35, 47

B
Bagby, George W. 91
Balcony Falls 31, 109
Bald Eagle 60
Baldwin, Loammi 5
Baltimore and Ohio Railroad 6
Batteau Festival 77
Batteaux 4, 5, 71, 76
Battery Creek 111
Beaver Creek 119
Beaverdam 151
Bent Creek 125
Bethel 58
Beyer, Edward 39
Big Island 110, 111
Big Sandy River 7
Bird, Henry D. 41
Blackwater Creek 32, 55, 57, 116
Blackwater Creek aqueduct 62, 67
Bleak House 45, 63
Blue Ridge Canal 7, 31, 36
Blue Ridge Dam 18, 37, 39, 109
Blue Ridge Gorge 7, 54
Blue Ridge Mountains 2, 42
Blue Ridge Parkway 111
Blue Ridge Parkway lock 60
Blue Ridge Rail Road 35, 43
Blue Ridge Turnpike 7
Board of Public Works. *See* Virginia Board of Public Works
Bolling Hall 13
Bolling, William 13, 15, 17, 19, 23, 29, 30
Bondurant, Thomas M. 37
Bosher 156
Bosher's Dam 26
Boyd, Edmunds & Co. 56, 73, 74
Boyd, James M. 74
Bremo Bluff 139
Bremo Creek, Big 138, 139, 140
Bremo Plantation 29
Briggs, Isaac 5
Bristol 45
Buchanan 3, 11, 22, 25, 35, 38, 39, 43, 44, 60, 71, 102
Butchard, Hester 66
Byrd Creek 144, 145
Byrd Park Pump House 159

C
Cabell, Dr. George 54
Cabell, Joseph C. 7, 8, 9, 12, 15, 19, 21, 22, 23, 28, 29, 30, 31, 32, 33, 34, 35, 37, 53, 54, 57, 67, 73
Campbell County 25, 54

CANAL BOAT CAPTAINS
Armsworthy 79, 80, 81, 82, 83, 84, 85
Ash 79, 80, 81, 82, 83, 84
Bailey (Baily) 79, 80, 81, 82, 83
Baldly 82
Beale 80
Bland 81
Branham 79
Brown 82, 83, 84
Charles 89
Childress 81, 82, 83, 84, 85
Clark (Clarke) 80, 81, 82, 83, 84, 85
Cloar (Cloas) 80, 81
Couch 82, 83, 84
Cowell 79, 80
Crouch 80, 85
Crump 83
Crumpacker (Crumpecker) 79, 80, 84, 85
Devigny (Devinney, Deviny) 79, 83, 84, 85
Dixon 85
Dolan 82, 83, 84
Doughty 80, 81, 82, 83
Eubank 79, 80, 82, 83, 84
Fields 79, 80, 81, 82, 83, 84
Fourqurean 83
Goodwin 80, 82, 83, 84
Grant 80, 81, 82, 83
Graves 79
Harrington 79, 80, 81, 82, 83, 84
Huckstep 80
Hull 73
Huntley 73
Jameison (Jemison) 79, 80, 81
Jenks 80, 82
King 79, 80
Lewis 79
Lilly 79, 80
Locket (Lockett) 79, 80, 81, 82, 83, 84
McGriffin (McCriffin, McGiffin) 79, 80, 81
Minor 80
Murrill 82
Nelson 85
Noell 81
Oberson 81
O'Connor (O'Conor) 82, 83
Orbeson (Orberson) 82, 83, 84
Overton 84
Pamplin (Pamphlin) 79, 80, 81, 82, 83
Pellet 79, 80, 81, 82, 83, 84, 85
Perkins 79
Peters 79, 80, 82, 83, 84
Phelps 81, 82, 83
Pryor 83, 84
Puryear 80
Quarles 80, 81, 82, 83, 84, 85
Roberts 83, 84
Shaw 85
Snedaker (Snediker) 79, 80, 84
Sneed 81
Spiller 81
Staton 79, 80, 81, 82
Taylor 79, 80, 82, 83, 85
Trent 84, 85
Wilson 79, 80

CANAL BOATS
Abingdon (*Abington*) 82, 83, 84, 85
Ben Franklin 81
Buchanan 57, 79, 80, 81, 82, 83, 84, 85
Champion 80, 81
Claytor & Burton (*Clayton & Burton*) 79, 80, 81, 82, 83, 84
Columbia 79, 82, 83, 84, 85
Commerce 79, 82
Davy Crockett (*David Crockett*) 57, 75, 80, 81, 82, 83
Elizabeth 79, 80, 83, 84
Enterprise (*Enterprize*) 79, 80, 81
Exchange 79, 81
Experiment 80, 82, 83, 84
Farmer 80, 82, 83, 84, 85
Flying Lucy 57, 79, 80, 82
Gabriel Tar (*Gabriel Tarr*) 82, 83, 84, 85
General Harrison 30, 53, 80, 81, 82, 83, 84, 85
Governor McDowell 33, 58
Harvey 89
Highlander 79, 80, 81, 82, 83, 84
Holker 80, 81
Jack Downing 79, 80, 82
James Madison 79, 80, 82, 83, 84
John Marshall 56, 65, 73
John Randolph 57, 75, 79, 80, 82, 83, 84
Jones 85
Joseph Cabell 78
Joseph C. Cabell 30, 56, 73, 78, 79, 80, 81, 82, 83
Josephine 57, 79, 80, 81, 82, 83, 84
Kanawha 57, 79, 80, 82, 84
Lady of the Lake 57, 82, 83
Lynchburg 57, 79, 80, 81, 82, 83, 84
Marshall 63, 65, 72
Mohawk 80, 81, 82, 83, 84, 85

Mountaineer 79, 80
Mount Vernon 33, 58
Ohio 57, 79, 80, 81
Old Dominion 57, 79, 80, 81, 82, 83, 84, 85
Old Virginia 57, 79, 80, 82, 83, 85
Pig Iron 57, 84, 85
Pioneer 79, 80, 81, 82, 83, 84, 85
Pocahontas (*Pocohontas*) 57, 80, 81, 82, 83
Raleigh 79, 80
Red Bird 57, 82, 83, 84
Richmond 57, 79, 80, 82, 83, 84
Tennessee 57, 79, 80, 81, 82, 83
The General Harrison 73
Union 80, 82
Victoria 79
Virginia 80
William H. Harrison 74
Wm. L. Lancaster 79, 80, 81, 82, 83, 84
Canal boats, dimensions 73
Cartersville 39, 145
Cement mill 37, 109
Cement mine 19, 107
Charleston, WV 7
Charlottesville 4
Chesapeake and Ohio Railway 6, 12, 14, 29, 33, 35, 37, 42, 48, 66
Chesapeake Bay 2
Chinn, E. L. 78
Chittenden, W. B. 14, 36, 37
Christian, W. Asbury 66, 73
Civil War 14, 47, 49, 63
Clifton Forge 42, 44, 49, 65, 66
Cocke, John Hartwell 29
Coleman Falls 112
Columbia 73, 142
Composite lock 20
Cooley, Ariel 4
Covington 2, 4, 7, 11, 21, 22, 38, 39, 42, 44
Covington and Ohio 42
Cowpasture River 2
Craighill, Major W. P. 47
Craig's Creek 43, 44
Crow's Ferry 3
Crozet, Claudius 5, 6, 7, 9, 22, 42
Culvert construction 24
Cumberland, Maryland 35, 37
Cushaw 60

D
Dabney, Albert Gallatin 57
Daniel, Elvira "Ellie" 14, 23, 54
Daniel's Island 54, 63
Daniel, William Jr. 62
Daniel, William Sr. 14, 54
Davenport, Isaac Jr. 74
Davies, Mary Elizabeth 58
Davies, Mayo 58
Dead Man's Hill 158
Divisions, Canal 11
Dolan, Kinnier & Co. 53, 73, 75
Dunlaps Creek 4

E
Eagle Rock 98
Ecole Polytechnique 6
Edmond, Robert 74
Ellet, Charles Jr. 11, 12, 14, 17, 20, 21, 22, 23, 36, 42, 54
Ellis, Thomas H. 43, 78
Erie Canal 4, 5, 6, 9, 21, 42, 44
Erie, Lake 6
Ewell, Professor 38

F
Fishing Creek 56
Floods 18, 32, 33, 37, 38, 42, 45, 48, 54, 56, 57, 58, 60, 63, 65, 72, 81
Fort Pitt 2
Fredonian mill 15
Free blacks 38
Freshet. *See* Floods

G
Gala 97
Gallatin, Albert 4
Galt's Mill 10, 28, 121
Gauley River 2
Genito Creek 152
Gerberding, C. O. 36, 37
Gill, Edward H. 22, 32, 54, 58, 61
Gill, Washington 55, 58
Gilmore Mills 105
Gladstone 124, 125
Glasgow 18, 107
Grant's Dam 159
Great Basin, Richmond 160
Great Lakes 6
Greenbrier River 2, 5
Gwynn Dam 99
Gwynn, Walter 29, 35, 36, 37, 38, 39, 41, 42, 43

H
Hague's 29
Hardware River 137
Harris, James M. 48, 62
Hatton Ferry 135
Hawkins, Leighman 88, 89
Haxall Canal 160
Haxall, Theodore vii, 91
Hollins Mill Dam 57
Horseford Creek 55
Howardsville 132
Hudson River 6
Huntington, WV 7
Hurt's Mill 56, 62
Hurt, Stephen C. 62
Hutton, William R. 48

I
Imboden, John D. 7
Immigrants.
See Labor, immigrant
Indian Rock 60

J
Jackson River 2
Jackson, Stonewall 63, 72
James River 1, 2, 3, 4, 11, 14, 34, 53, 54, 55
James River and Kanawha Company 3, 7, 8, 9, 14, 15, 34, 43, 45, 73
James River Canal 6, 38
James River Cement Company 37
James River Company 3, 4, 5, 6, 7, 47
Jarvis, Mr. 38
Joshua Falls 26, 54, 73, 78, 119
Judith Creek 60
Judith Dam 29, 38, 40, 67, 115

K
Kanawha, Great Falls of the 2, 5, 11, 21
Kanawha River 1, 2, 4, 7, 11, 22, 53, 54
Kanawha Turnpike 7, 41
King, J.S. 55
Kinsey, Charles 12, 18

L
Labor, free black 38
Labor, immigrant 27, 28, 29, 38, 67
Labor, slave 27, 29, 38, 40, 41, 61, 67 40
Lake, William 19, 32

Latrobe, Benjamin 47
Lewis, William S. 13
Lexington 30, 45, 65, 66, 72, 74
Licking Hole Creek 149
Lipper, Mr. 23
Livermore, Daniel 11, 17
Locher Cement Plant 18
Locher, Charles 37
Looneys Creek 3
Lorraine, Edward 36, 43, 45, 47, 48, 58, 63
Lynchburg 5, 7, 8, 11, 15, 18, 21, 22, 23, 25, 27, 29, 30, 31, 35, 38, 43, 45, 48, 49, 53, 54, 56, 57, 58, 71, 73, 75, 76, 93, 115, 116
Lynchburg and Danville Railroad 65
Lynchburg Virginian 35, 43

M
Mahan, Professor 38
Maiden's Adventure 19, 21, 28, 151
Maiden's Adventure Dam 6, 11, 26
Marshall, John, Chief Justice 4, 8, 44
Marshall Tunnel 44, 100
Mason, John Y. 37, 38, 41, 42, 43
Mason Tunnel 44, 101
Maury River. *See* North
Mayo-Davies 63
McAlpine 38
McFarlan, Alexander B. 37
McGehee, Minnie Lee vi, vii
McNeill, William G. 6, 22
Meggert, Frank 28
Midway Mills 128, 129
Montgomerie, Hugh 74
Moore, Thomas 5
Morris Canal 12
Mosby, Charles L. 53
Mount Athos 13, 25, 54, 119, 120

N
Natural Bridge Station 106
New River 2, 5
North (Maury) 23, 36, 37, 41, 49, 108
North River Line 45
North River Navigation Company 45
Norwood 127
N&W 59

O

Ohio River 1, 2, 3, 6, 11, 21, 34, 35, 37, 41, 42, 45, 53
Opossum Creek 67, 118
Orange & Alexandria Railroad ix, 62
Owens Creek 126, 127

P

Packet boat. *See* Canal boats
Paddle wheels 33, 58
Padget, Frank 29
Pattonsburg 11
Pennsylvania Canal 18, 21
Percival, John 15, 54
Petersburg 43, 61
Petersburg and Roanoke Railroad 41
Philadelphia 18, 21
Phoenix Foundry 57
Piedmont Mills 56
Pigeon Creek 67
Pittsburgh 2, 18, 21
Point of Honor 14, 54, 67
Point Pleasant 2, 11
Porridge Creek 122, 123
Portsmouth and Roanoke Railroad 35
Potomac River 6, 14
Proffit, Matthew 66
Pudding Hill 122

Q

Quarry Falls 60, 106

R

Railroad 34, 61
Rensselaer School 6
Reusens 58, 60, 61, 65
Reusens Dam 38, 115

Richmond 4, 7, 8, 11, 18, 19, 21, 25, 27, 28, 30, 35, 38, 40, 43, 47, 49, 53, 57, 63, 65, 66, 71, 73, 75, 77, 78, 89, 157, 158, 159, 160, 161
Richmond & Allegheny 48, 59, 65, 66, 101
Richmond & Danville Railroad 45, 47
Rivanna Navigation 38
Rivanna River 3, 49, 142
Rivermont House 67
Riverside Park 65, 72
Roanoke Rail Road Company 35
Roberts, Mr. 38
Robertson, John 13, 15, 17, 25
Robertson, Wyndham 13
Rockfish River 132
Roebling, John 14, 25
Rope ferry 25, 54, 119

S

Salt Creek 114
Sandy & Beaver Canal 22, 25
Scandal 37
Scott's Mill 16
Scott's Mill Dam 16, 116
Scottsville 11, 73, 92, 135
Shenandoah Valley 2
Shepperson & Co. 73
Sheridan's raid 63
Ship lock 161
Slack water navigation 5
Slave labor. *See* Labor, slave
Slaves 27, 29
Sluices 4
Smeaton, John 6
Snow Creek 110
Snowden 28

Southside Railroad 43, 45
Stapleton 122, 123
Steamboats 33
Steam propelled 33, 58
Stein, Albert 53
Stephenson, George 6
Stockton and Darlington Railroad 6
Stokes, Goochland County 91
Storms 31
Stovall Creek 121
Stovall Creek Aqueduct 10
Sugar Tree Creek 67

T

Tidewater 4
Tidewater Connection 4, 38, 40, 43, 160, 161
Tinsley, Nelson 18, 37
Tioga and Chemung Railroad 17
Tobacco 58
Toler, Richard H. 35
Trout, William vi, vii, 77, 96
Tuckahoe Creek 155, 156
Turnbull, Colonel 38
Tye River 11, 26, 54, 127
Tyler, John 37

U

United States Topographical Engineers 38

V

Varney's Falls 104, 105
Virginia and Tennessee Railroad 45, 61, 67
Virginia Board of Public Works 5, 42
Virginia Central Railroad 42

Virginia General Assembly 3, 7, 17, 31, 35, 36, 37, 42, 43, 54
Virginia Military Institute 74
Virginia Nail and Iron Works 61

W

Walker, Ezra 41
Walton, D. W. 43
War of 1812 5
Washington, George 1, 2, 53
Wasp Rock 60, 103
Waterworks canal, Lynchburg 33
Waterworks dam, Lynchburg 16, 18, 26, 33, 54, 55, 60, 63, 65, 66, 67
Waterworks, Lynchburg 53
Weldon, North Carolina 35
Weston, William 6, 9
West Point 6, 35, 38, 43
White Sulphur Springs 5, 22
Wilkinson, James A. 65, 72
Wilkinson, James P. 65, 72
William and Mary, The College of 38, 43
Wing dams 4
Wingina 128, 129
Wright, Benjamin 5, 7, 8, 9, 11, 12, 14, 17, 23, 32
Wright, Simon W. 11, 17